For Davi[...]
on you[...] [...]day,

with love,

Muriel & Doug

CAR MAINTENANCE MADE EASY

CAR
MAINTENANCE
MADE EASY

IAN WARD

ORBIS PUBLISHING·LONDON

PICTURE ACKNOWLEDGMENTS

L.J. Caddell/Orbis 8, 30A; Car Mechanics Magazine 10, 53A-B; Champion 17B-I; Ferodo 49A; FIAT 29; GKN 34, 47; R.A. Hall 31A; Harlequin Studio/Orbis 7B; James Neill Ltd 6, 7A; M. Lawrence/Orbis 2, 12A, 16, 22B, 23, 25B, 26A, 39B–D, 48B, 51B–E; Lucas 19, 60; Marelli 17A; Milleruote 30B, 31B, 32, 33, 48C; Orbis Publishing 14B, 15, 18, 20, 38, 39A, 40, 41, 43, 46B-D, 48A, 49B, 50, 51A, 52, 58A, 61; Papetti 21, 28; Popular Motoring Magazine 12B, 13, 14A, 45, 46A, 58B-C, 59; Quattroruote 22A; P. Revere 54, 55, 56, 57; SU Carburettors 26B, 27; Zenith Carburettors 24, 25a.

Title page illustration: connecting the headlamp (sealed beam unit) of a Ford Escort

Printed in Czechoslovakia

ISBN 0 85613 043 5
50131

CONTENTS

TOOLS

An adequate tool kit need not be large and costly. We may start with the most common form of fastening, the screw thread. The screw or bolt head may be slotted, to take a screw-driver; shaped as a hexagon, calling for a spanner; or rebated; to accept a key, commonly an Allen key.

The basic types of screwdriver are straight bladed or cross-headed, such as Phillips or Posidrive. Always use the correct type. The blade should fit tightly without overlapping or being small enough to damage the slot. Ratchet screwdrivers are designed for speed of operation and impact screwdrivers are used for loosening stubborn screws.

Hexagon headed nuts or bolts call for one of a variety of spanners. BS and Whitworth sizes are based on the thread diameter, while UNF, AF and metric sizes are measured across the flats of the nut or bolt head. Most modern cars use metric bolts, but older machines may use one or more of the alternatives. Electrical components commonly use very small BA nuts, sized by number. A range of perhaps a dozen spanner sizes,

Below: tools for virtually every occasion or eventuality. This impressive array gives some idea of the vast range which is available, although a more modest selection should suit most amateur mechanics

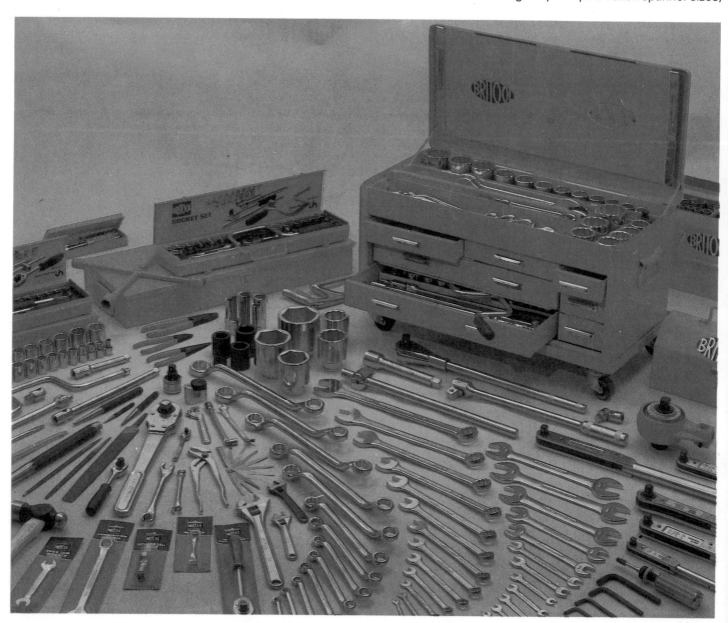

Above: a 'spider' wheelbrace is extremely useful for the workshop, as it makes wheelnut removals a quick and easy task; it is almost essential if one is to deal simply with nuts that have been tightened by air wrenches at a tyre-fitting specialists

Below: an impact screwdriver, preferably with interchangeable bits, as here, is invaluable for use on stubborn screws

carefully chosen, copes with most jobs.

For awkward places, offset spanners, flat ring spanners or 'obstruction' spanners are available. Other spanners vary in shape from make to make and shopping around may make a difficult job easier, as may 'adapting' a spanner for a particular problem.

Adjustable spanners should only be used where a fixed jaw spanner is not available and lockable grips, pliers and wrenches should only be used as a last resort. Where space is restricted, box spanners or sockets are the solution. Box spanners are usually double-ended and are turned by a bar; they are also available in cranked form.

Sockets can be turned by a straight or cranked bar, a ratchet, a brace or a torque wrench. With extension bars and universal joints they are among the most versatile of tools. For the serious mechanic, a torque wrench and sockets allow tightening to specified loads and safeguard against stripped threads and uneven tightening.

For recessed-head bolts, Allen keys can be bought in sets of commonly used metric or Imperial sizes.

Almost every car has some part which needs a special puller. Before using any puller, care must be taken to see that all fixings have been removed. If excessive force is needed, something has probably been overlooked, and further damage can be caused.

A butane blowlamp can double for soldering, but for delicate jobs an electric soldering iron with a pointed bit should be obtained.

A selection of pliers, hammers and punches is useful. One standard and one long-nosed pair of pliers, plus a pair of circlip pliers are a good selection. A self-grip wrench can be used, with care, as a clamp, or, fixed on a bench mounting, as a small vice. Wire cutters and strippers may also earn their keep as badly made connections could lead to further electrical problems.

Carefully used, the appropriate hammer is more than a last resort, perhaps with a punch or small chisel, but a good rule is never to use a heavier hammer than is necessary. A double-sided points file, double-sided flat file and a round file are further good investments, as are a hand or electric drill and bits.

Some specialised tools (a valve spring compressor, feeler gauges and ignition timing light for instance) can avoid expensive damage — the correct tool is usually cheaper than new parts. So, before starting on repairs or adjustments, it is advisable to ensure that any specialised tool required is at hand.

A large strong toolbox completes the basic essentials. A really good set of tools can be built up over a long period but can pay for itself in a single major overhaul.

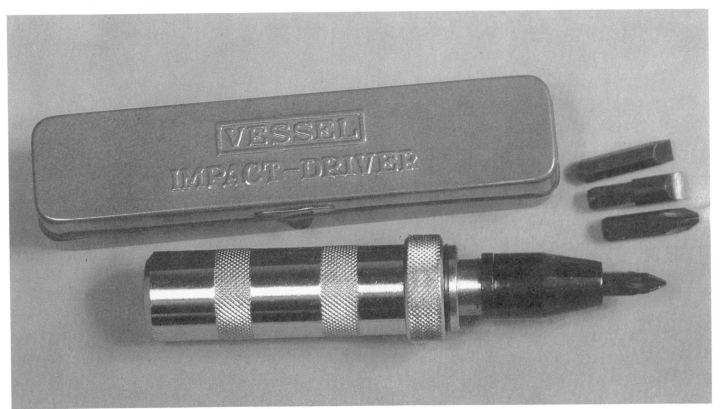

SERVICING

This section explains the tasks necessary to keep a car running smoothly and properly. It includes regular checks which must be made, together with details of servicing procedures which must be carried out at regular intervals. These intervals should be checked with the manufacturer's handbook, as should specific settings and capacities.

REGULAR CHECKS

Every car, no matter how well made and sophisticated it may be, requires regular servicing in order to keep it in good running order and prolong its life. A well maintained vehicle will last many more years than one which is expected to run with no more assistance than a few tanks-full of petrol and an occasional oil-check.

Some parts of the engine need occasional checking, such as the air filter (near right) and the carburettor (far right)

We give below some helpful hints for daily and weekly checks and procedures; if these are followed faithfully you will be amply rewarded.

CHECKING OIL LEVEL

Until you get to know the rate of oil consumption of your car, this level should be checked every day or so. Remove the dipstick, situated on the side of the engine (usually at the front of a transverse engine), and note the position of the oil, relative to the 'max' and 'min' marks. If the level is below maximum, then oil should be added, through the cap on top of the engine, until the deficit is made up.

Do not overfill the sump (this is where the oil is stored) because any excess is usually blown out of the crankcase breather, making a mess of the engine and its compartment.

CHECKING HYDRAULIC FLUID LEVELS

Most cars today have hydraulically operated clutches and brakes — the pedal operates a piston in a cylinder, which pushes fluid down a pipe to another piston and cylinder operating the clutch or brake.

If the fluid level in the reservoirs, usually situated under the 'bonnet' and near the pedals, drops appreciably, then the system must be checked, for this indicates a leak. However, if the level only changes by a very small amount over a period of several weeks or months, then this is probably due to clutch/brake-wear and evaporation.

The cylinders should be topped up with the correct grade of hydraulic fluid (see maker's handbook), until the level is up to the top or to a specially marked line.

CHECKING WATER LEVEL AND ANTI-FREEZE

It is always best to check the level of coolant in the radiator when the engine is cold. This avoids water and steam squirting out and scalding you. If it is necessary to do this under hot conditions, then remove the radiator cap very slowly, allowing the pressure to escape, before lifting the cap off completely.

As winter approaches, you should fill the engine cooling system with an anti-freeze solution — a 1:3 ratio of anti-freeze to water is usual.

Drain the cooling system by loosening the taps normally found on the bottom of the radiator and on the side of the cylinder block, then flush out the muck with a hosepipe. Having closed the taps, pour in the correct quantity of a good anti-freeze and top up with water. Remember to check the water level after a few moments running.

When your radiator is filled with anti-freeze, any topping up should be carried out using a similar solution, to maintain the concentration.

Check the condition of the radiator hoses regularly, to make sure that they are not perished or leaking at the joints. If any of them seem to be soft, or are impregnated with oil, they should be replaced before they fail.

CHECKING AND TOPPING UP THE BATTERY

The distilled water used in a lead-acid battery evaporates in use — the rate of evaporation depends on the amount of use and on the outside temperature. Batteries mounted under the bonnet tend to lose more water than those inside the car or in the boot. The level should be up to a marked line, or to a point where it just covers the plates in each cell. Most modern batteries have a quick-fill arrangement, whereby all the cells can be filled at once by pouring distilled water into a trough. Older batteries have individual cells which have to be checked and topped up one at a time.

CHECKING TYRE PRESSURES AND CONDITION

Modern pneumatic tyres maintain their pressure for long periods, but it is worth checking them every week or so. A tyre pressure gauge can be purchased cheaply from an accessory shop and it is worth having one of these as the accuracy of garage gauges is variable and dubious. By all means use the compressed air supply at the local garage, to save effort, but preferably use your own gauge.

If possible, carry out the check when the tyres are cold, as the air pressure increases as temperature rises. Don't forget to check the spare; if you don't you may be caught out if you ever have a puncture.

When you are checking pressures, have a look at the condition of the tyres: make sure there is plenty of tread — 1 mm is the legal minimum in Britain — and that the sidewalls have no cuts or bulges and remove any large stones from the tread, using a blunt screwdriver or suchlike, rather than a sharp knife!

WASHING THE CAR

This sounds a simple procedure, but it is possible to damage the paint if care is not exercised. If the car is not too dirty, hot water should be all that is required for the job. Special shampoo, or ordinary washing-up liquid will be needed for grease, traffic grime, etc — this will usually remove any polish previously applied to the paint.

Use a sponge or soft brush and apply plenty of water, making sure that no grit is rubbed into the surface. Having rinsed off any detergent or soap, use a dampened chamois leather to wipe off the remaining water, squeezing (not wringing) the leather to remove the water and rinsing it.

If the paint is still not shiny, then a haze remover must be employed. This is applied like a polish and is a mild abrasive. Some polishes contain haze remover, but if you don't use one of these, then you should use a good wax polish afterwards.

Don't let any polish get on the windscreen or on the wiper blades: poor vision in wet weather will result.

Brightwork should come clean with water and soap, and wax polish takes off a great deal of the stubborn dirt. As a last resort metal polish should be used sparingly.

Carpets can be cleaned with a stiff brush, or they can be removed and vacuum cleaned — small 12-volt cylinder cleaners are available for use with the carpets in place. Household carpet shampoo may be applied if dirt will not brush off. Plastic or leather seats can be cleaned with a damp cloth, but ground-in dirt will need soap or special upholstery cleaner. Cloth seats, too, will need a special cleaner, which may also be used on a cloth headlining. This substance is usually sprayed on, scrubbed in and wiped off.

LOOKING AFTER WIPERS AND WASHERS

Check your windscreen wiper blades, every so often. If the edges are rippled, then they must be replaced if adequate wiping is to be maintained. As the arms age, the joints become loose and the springs weak. The first may allow the metal parts to touch ths screen and scratch it, while the second will lead to the blades leaving the screen at high speed. New springs can be purchased from accessory shops.

Washer jets can clog, but a pin is usually sufficient to clear the blockage. Special additives are available to dissolve dirt and keep the jets clean, and these should be used in preference to the more convenient washing-up liquid, which will result in jet blockage.

CHANGING OILS

ENGINE OIL

Lubricating oils are becoming more sophisticated all the time. It is not all that many years ago that engine oil was single grade only and contained no additives at all. In those days, it was recommended that different grades of oil be used for summer and winter. The lack of detergents in the oils meant that sludge formed within the engine and frequent oil changes were necessary.

Today, engine oil contains many additives to make it more effective and to improve its high-temperature stability. It is no longer necessary to use summer and winter grades, since the advent of multigrade oils means that the two grades can be combined in one oil.

However, no matter how efficient the oil, it will eventually deteriorate and will have to be changed. The interval between oil changes varies, nowadays, between 3000 and 6000 miles, depending on the make of the car and the state of tune of the engine (it is usual for highly stressed power units to require more frequent oil changes than the lazy ones).

As wear takes place in the engine, metal particles find their way into the oil. These particles could do devastating damage if allowed to stay in the oil, so they are filtered out. After several thousand miles the filter will begin to block; this is when it should be changed. In many types of car, the filter is changed with the same frequency as the oil, while in others the requirement is one filter change to every other oil change.

There are two types of oil filter; the throwaway type and the replaceable-element type. Throwaway oil filters are complete units which screw direct into the engine; they cannot be taken apart and so they have to be replaced as a whole. Replaceable-element types consist of a canister, into which the filter element is placed. Instead of changing the whole assembly, the element can be replaced.

The procedure for changing engine oil is fairly standard for most cars, the differences being in the positioning of the important parts such as the drain plug and the oil filter.

The first job is to start the engine and run it until it is warm. This thins the oil so that it will run out of the drain hole more readily than if cold. Having done this, the drain plug should be unscrewed. This plug is situated somewhere near the lowest point on

Above: two different types of oil filter, the throwaway type (left) and the replaceable-element type

Right: the engine oil drain plug is usually situated at or near the lowest point of the sump. It is best to warm the engine before draining the oil, so as to thin it as much as possible

the sump (at the bottom of the engine) and is usually recognisable as a plug. Most cars have a standard hexagonal head on the drain plug allowing the plug to be undone with a normal spanner. Several makes, however, use an Allen screw or a square-socket plug, which cannot be removed without an Allen key or a special sump plug spanner.

Before the plug is removed completely, a container, large enough to contain a sump-full of oil, should be placed in the best position to catch all that oil. While the sump is draining, the filter should be removed (if the job is due). The throwaway type is removed by turning the whole body of the canister in an anti-clockwise direction. Some filters have a hexagonal knob pressed into the end of the canister, so that a spanner can be employed to assist with this removal. Should the filter refuse to move and be the type without a hexagon, it may be possible to turn the canister by tapping it in the correct direction with a cold chisel and hammer. Otherwise, a strap wrench should be used. Once this type of filter has been removed, it is only necessary to clean any spilled oil from around the seating before fitting the new unit. A new sealing ring should always be used, but this is usually already affixed to the filter casing. Even if the canister

Right: there is usually a rubber sealing ring to be replaced when changing a 'refillable' oil filter; the new seal will be supplied with the filter element and care must be taken to ensure that it is fitted correctly

does have a hexagon, a spanner should not be used during the refitting process, since it is possible to overtighten the unit and damage the seal, the thread or both. Hand pressure is enough to prevent leaks.

The replaceable-element oil filter is removed by unscrewing the bolt which passes either through the filter casing into the engine or through something like the oil-pump body into the filter casing. Once the bolt has been fully unscrewed, the canister may need tapping to free the bond between it, the sealing ring and the seating. Preparation should be made to catch anything up to a pint of oil contained in the filter canister. With the filter off, the element should be tipped out of its casing, making sure that any plates, springs or washers are retained for use with the new element.

After the canister has been washed out with paraffin or petrol, the new element should be fitted with the various bits and pieces in the correct places. The sealing ring is most commonly fitted to a groove in the oil-filter seating and this ring should be replaced.

The filter casing should be refitted to is mounting carefully, so that it is seating evenly on the sealing ring. Ideally, the fixing bolt should be tightened to the torque shown in the maker's literature.

By the time the filter has been replaced, the oil should have drained out. The plug should be cleaned, especially if it is of the magnetic type, and replaced. The correct amount of oil can now be poured in through the filler hole, usually situated on the cam or rocker cover.

Finally, the engine should be run and the joint between the filter and the engine checked for leaks. If there is a leak, the filter should be reseated. When the oil has run back down the sump, the level should be checked on the dipstick to confirm that the correct amount of lubricant has been added.

It is a good idea to wash out the lubrication system with special flushing oil. This becomes really worthwhile if the old oil is heavily contaminated with metal particles and sludge. The precedure should be carried out before the filter is changed. After draining the old oil, the plug should be replaced and the sump half filled with flushing oil. The engine should be run at fast idle until it is warm again, and the flushing oil should be drained. The filter can now be changed and the procedure continued as before.

GEARBOX AND REAR-AXLE OIL

It is unusual, in modern cars, for gearbox or rear-axle oil-draining facilities to be provided. All that is necessary is an occasional top-up. As with engine oils, transmission oils have improved a great deal and several manufacturers consider that the oil will last as long as the gearbox or rear axle.

In order to check the level of the oil, the level plug/filler should be removed. This is usually situated on the side of the gearbox or on the reat of the differential housing and involves some contortions on the part of the mechanic. If topping-up is required, a flexible tube is usually the best weapon with which to attack the problem. Some cars, especially those with automatic transmission, have a gearbox filler tube under the bonnet; this simplifies matters considerably

If the gearbox or rear axle has a draining facility, the plug is usually situated at the lowest point, in the same way as on the sump.

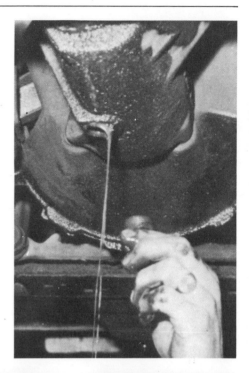

Right: it is unusual today for gearboxes to require oil changes, but if they do, the plug is usually situated on the bottom of the casing

Right: transmission oil is most commonly supplied in flexible plastic bottles, with a similar spout, to facilitate gearbox or rear axle filling

GREASING AND OILING

LUBRICATION
ref: greasing and oiling

Below: a lubrication chart for a Jaguar E-type; although this is rather a special car, there is nothing odd about its lubrication procedures or points

Several motor manufacturers have done away with grease points on the chassis of their products, advertising these wares as being 'lubricated for life'. However, in some cases, this life turns out to be rather short, because the lubricant in, for example, a steering track-rod end has leaked away.

Of course, servicing costs are reduced, but in the long run extra expense is incurred by the replacement of these worn parts.

The problem with cars that do still need greasing and oiling is that they tend to be neglected. Some owners take their cars to a garage at regular intervals for this servicing to be carried out, but others, who perhaps have a little less money to spare, are inclined to 'leave well alone'. This, of course, is like avoiding the dentist because one's teeth are not hurting: in the end they have to come out.

Greasing and oiling a car is, with few exceptions, a simple task which takes only an hour or so. The only tools required are a grease gun and an oil gun (the same gun will usually suffice, although it makes the job very messy).

Most joints and bearings can be lubricated with an all-purpose grease, such as Castrolease LM, although some parts, especially on older cars, may need special-purpose preparations. Oils are a little more varied. The greatest users of oil, other than the engine, are the gearbox and the final-drive unit. If power steering is fitted, this too will need oil. The most common lubricant for manual gearboxes and final drives is hypoid oil, developed specially for the extreme pressures developed between gear teeth. Automatic gearboxes and power-steering units, however, usually require a special type of their own.

Nowadays, some front-wheel-drive units, such as that in the British Leyland Mini, use a common lubricant for the engine, the gearbox and the final drive, this lubricant being engine oil, which simplifies matters.

Unfortunately, it is quite common for one grade of oil to be recommended for use in the gearbox, while another is needed for the final-drive unit (for example EP80 for the gearbox and EP90 for the final drive). This can lengthen the job, if a gun is needed, because the oils will have to be changed.

A normal (non-assisted) steering unit usually makes use of hypoid oil, although, in the same way as gearboxes and final drives, servicing intervals are usually very long.

Before attempting to lubricate any of the compenents, it is wise, therefore to check the manufacturer's literature for the correct types and grades of

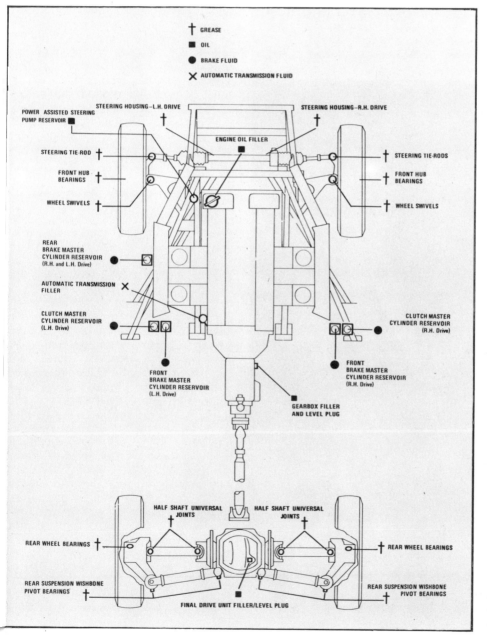

† GREASE
■ OIL
● BRAKE FLUID
✕ AUTOMATIC TRANSMISSION FLUID

STEERING HOUSING–L.H. DRIVE
STEERING HOUSING–R.H. DRIVE
POWER ASSISTED STEERING PUMP RESERVOIR
ENGINE OIL FILLER
STEERING TIE-ROD
STEERING TIE-RODS
FRONT HUB BEARINGS
FRONT HUB BEARINGS
WHEEL SWIVELS
WHEEL SWIVELS
REAR BRAKE MASTER CYLINDER RESERVOIR (R.H. and L.H. Drive)
AUTOMATIC TRANSMISSION FILLER
CLUTCH MASTER CYLINDER RESERVOIR (L.H. Drive)
CLUTCH MASTER CYLINDER RESERVOIR (R.H. Drive)
FRONT BRAKE MASTER CYLINDER RESERVOIR (L.H. Drive)
FRONT BRAKE MASTER CYLINDER RESERVOIR (R.H. Drive)
GEARBOX FILLER AND LEVEL PLUG
HALF SHAFT UNIVERSAL JOINTS
HALF SHAFT UNIVERSAL JOINTS
REAR WHEEL BEARINGS
REAR WHEEL BEARINGS
REAR SUSPENSION WISHBONE PIVOT BEARINGS
REAR SUSPENSION WISHBONE PIVOT BEARINGS
FINAL DRIVE UNIT FILLER/LEVEL PLUG

lubricant. There is often a plate fixed under the bonnet (sometimes on the top of the engine), which lists these oils and greases. If the car is old, however, some of these makes and types may have been superseded.

A chart is shown of the lubrication points for the Jaguar E-type V12. This was by no means a standard car, but the chart gives a good indication of the typical components which require lubrication with either oil or grease.

The chart includes the reservoirs for the brake and clutch hydraulic systems. The fluid used in these circuits is not strictly a lubricant, but it can be used as such on any rubber parts which are inclined to squeak (such as suspension bushes). It is important that ordinary oil and grease are kept away from any rubber or plastic parts, unless otherwise recommended, as chemical action may occur and destroy the parts.

THE BEST TOOLS AND HOW TO USE THEM

Below: the best type of grease gun is the lever-action, high-pressure instrument, as it requires only one-handed operation and it tends to fit positively on to the grease nipple. These guns can be fitted with either firm spouts, as shown here, or flexible ones

Any grease/oil gun will do for most cars, but some types make more work for the user than is necessary and others can be very messy.

Car manufacturers have a habit of placing grease nipples and oil fillers where they cannot be reached without difficulty. For these the best type of gun is the lever-operated high-pressure instrument which can be operated with one hand. This type can

be fitted with a flexible spout, which can be attached firmly to each nipple, allowing the tool itself to be placed in a convenient position. Even the firm spouts are usually angled and allowed to swivel for the best angle of attack, and these, too, can be fixed to the nipples by means of a screw tip.

Easily accessible grease nipples can be attacked with the older pump-action gun, where the spout disappears into the handle/reservoir. The problem with this type is that leakage is likely to occur around the nipple unless the instrument is absolutely straight, since the spout is only a push-fit. What is more, the mechanical advantage is small compared with the long lever of the former type, so the pressure build-up is not as great.

Before any attempt is made to lubricate a component, via a nipple, that nipple should be thoroughly cleaned, in order to prevent the ingress of dirt and grit. If, after the grease gun has been attached, the lubricant fails to enter the nipple, then there is a good chance that the nipple is blocked.

The first course of action is to unscrew the offending part and clean it with petrol or paraffin. If, after this, grease will not pass through it, the ball valve (on the outside) should be depressed by means of something like a screwdriver. If all else fails, a new component will have to be fitted.

If on removal the grease nipple is found to be clear, then the component, into which the lubricant was supposed to go, will have to be dismantled and cleaned.

A lever-type grease gun can usually overcome any blockage problems, however, since it has enormous pressure and a good fluid seal to the nipple, preventing leakage.

It is not very often that a gun is needed for oil, since it is supplied in flexible bottles with flexible spouts. Occasionally, however, components have to be oiled through a nipple. Then the procedure is exactly as for grease.

SPARK PLUGS

Despite the fact that spark plugs carry out a straightforward and simple task, in that they cause the fuel/air mixture in an internal combustion engine to ignite, they require regular, careful attention to keep the engine running well. It is fairly obvious that a plug fouled with oil or carbon may fail to fire, but not so obvious that there is no black-and-white division between a spark plug working and not working.

Most car manufacturers recommend that spark plugs be cleaned and adjusted every five or six thousand miles and that they be changed every ten or twelve thousand. This is probably a good rule to go by, but different engines place differing stresses on spark plugs, as do different working conditions.

If the carburettor is not adjusted properly, this will undoubtedly lead to reduced plug life: a rich mixture will cause the formation of excessive carbon deposits, while a weak mixture will cause overheating and burning of the spark-plug electrodes. Although in the former case it is possible to clean off the deposits, it is very difficult to remove all foreign matter from the space between the plug body and the insulator. In the end, this build-up can lead to a short-circuit.

The solution, then, is to make sure that the carburettor is correctly set and

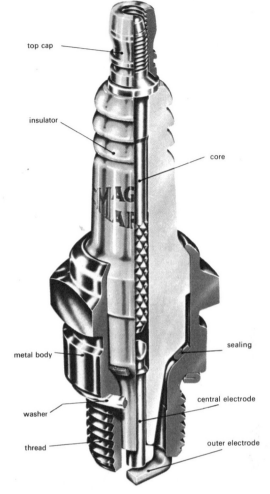

Right: a cutaway view of a spark plug with an internal air gap; the idea of this type of plug, now very rare, was to boost the spark at the electrodes

Below: from left to right in the top row, the pictures show a normal spark plug and ones fouled by carbon and damaged by overheating and pre-ignition; in the bottom row from left to right the pictures show oil fouling, heavy deposits due, perhaps, to excessive use of lubricant, impact damage to the insulator and abrasive erosion caused by excessive cleaning

17

to check the plug condition regularly — it is annoying, to say the least, when an engine starts misfiring on one or more cylinders, no matter how intermittently, and naturally this will spoil performance.

CLEANING

To most people, cleaning a spark plug involves no more than a quick scrub with a wire brush and, perhaps, a rub with a piece of emery cloth. In fact, the spark plug manufacturers will say that this is not sufficient to remove all contamination. The best way of cleaning a plug is to sand-blast it, since the sand can find its way into the gap we mentioned above. Nowadays, portable bead blasters are available quite cheaply so this cleaning method is open to all. However, the next best thing is to use hand tools. It is true that a wire brush is very useful, but it is also a help to make use of a thin, sharp object, such as a nail, to scrape out the plug body/insulator space.

In many cases, especially where a weak mixture has existed, a hard deposit will have been formed on the electrodes. This must be scraped off, not forgetting the underside of the side electrode. Finally, the electrodes should be thoroughly cleaned with a file (special points files can be obtained for this purpose). Experiments by one of the leading plug manufacturers, have shown that the voltage required to provide a spark in a wire-brushed plug is considerably higher than that required for one whose electrodes have been filed.

Right: it is essential to file the electrodes after cleaning the plug, even if a sand or bead-blasting machine is used, as this reduces the voltage required for a good spark

ADJUSTING

The gap between the electrodes should be checked by means of a feeler gauge (right) and adjusted, if necessary, with a special gapping tool (below)

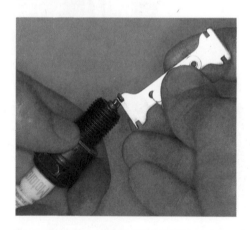

When the plug is completely clean, the gap should be set, taking care to bend only the side electrode. This contact should be adjusted by bending it as a whole, not by bending it in the middle, using a gap-adjusting tool.

The clearance between the two electrodes should be fixed at that recommended by the car manufacturer, by using a feeler gauge of the correct size. The gap will be correct when the weight of the gauge can just be supported by the friction between it and the electrodes.

Before replacing the spark plugs, the insulators, on the outside of the cylinder, should be cleaned, in order to prevent the voltage (around twenty thousand) from 'tracking' between the terminal and the nut.

With the plugs back in the engine and tightened to the recommended

torque, something which is especially important with an aluminium-alloy cylinder head, the plug caps should be cleaned before replacement. As with the plug insulators, deposits of dirt can lead to 'tracking', which in turn, will impair the efficiency of the engine.

HIGH TENSION LEADS

The high tension lead should be firmly connected to the plug caps, especially in the case of the suppressor type, which have carbon cores rather than wire ones. It is not uncommon for a gap to form in the carbon, which may eventually become too large for a spark to jump, resulting in a dud plug.

If the leads have to be replaced, it is better to fit the wire variety, together with new plug caps containing built-in suppressors. The likelihood of a fault is greatly reduced.

One final point, concerning the plugs and their leads; it pays to number the high-tension leads to correspond with the cylinder numbers (usually starting from one at the front of the engine). This precludes any chance of the leads being replaced in the wrong order.

We have dealt with the correct maintenance of spark plugs, showing how this is important to the running of an engine, but clean spark plugs will be no good without a distributor which is working correctly.

The exploded diagram shows how many parts go to making up a distributor, but fortunately most of these will continue indefinitely to function correctly. A small amount of regular attention will ensure that this part of the ignition system performs adequately.

Right: an exploded view of a Lucas distributor of the type with both centrifugal and vacuum advance mechanisms

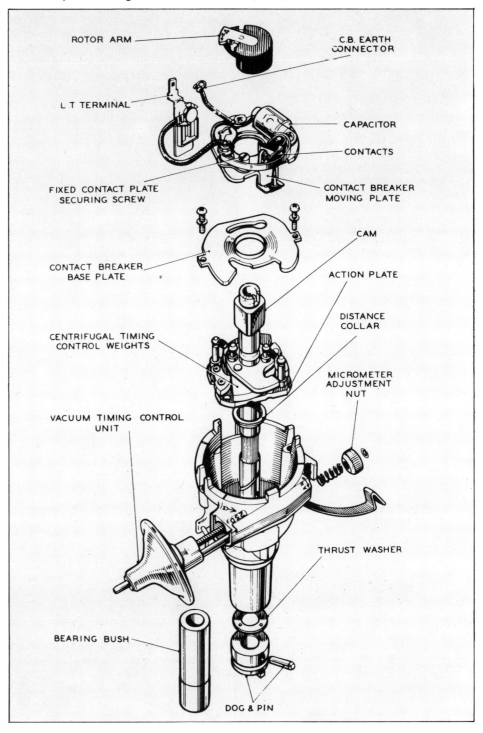

ROTOR ARM

C.B. EARTH CONNECTOR

L T TERMINAL

CAPACITOR

CONTACTS

FIXED CONTACT PLATE SECURING SCREW

CONTACT BREAKER MOVING PLATE

CONTACT BREAKER BASE PLATE

CAM

ACTION PLATE

CENTRIFUGAL TIMING CONTROL WEIGHTS

DISTANCE COLLAR

MICROMETER ADJUSTMENT NUT

VACUUM TIMING CONTROL UNIT

THRUST WASHER

BEARING BUSH

DOG & PIN

CONTACT BREAKERS

The contact breaker points require the most frequent servicing, because the plastic knob, which rests on the distributor camshaft, will wear and the points themselves are inclined slowly to burn. If the camshaft is lightly greased every few thousand miles, the wear will be cut to a minimum, but unless transistorised ignition is fitted the burning is unavoidable.

When greasing the camshaft, it is important not to apply too much lubricant, as any excess may find its way on to the points and cause a break in the electrical circuit. A smear is sufficient for a long period of running.

If the contact points were to wear evenly, the job of adjustment would be simple, but unfortunately they tend to wear into bumps and hollows.

ADJUSTMENT

Right: most distributors have the type of contact points system shown here; adjustment is carried out by first loosening the screw (arrowed) then moving the fixed point, by means of a screwdriver in the groove provided, until the correct gap — measured by a feeler gauge (right) — is obtained

Adjustment is normally carried out using a screwdriver and a feeler gauge. The fixed contact should be moved until the clearance between it and its moving partner is that specified by the manufacturer (when the gap is at its widest). The points should just nip the feeler without having to open to admit it.

If a knob is present on one of the contacts, it will be impossible to obtain a correct setting with a feeler gauge.

There are two courses of action: fit new points or grind the present ones flat. Let us deal with the latter course first.

Distributor points are hardened, so it is not at all easy to file them. The correct procedure is to grind them on a flat oil stone until both bump and dent are removed. Great care should be taken to ensure that the surfaces are kept flat and parallel, so that the points still meet properly.

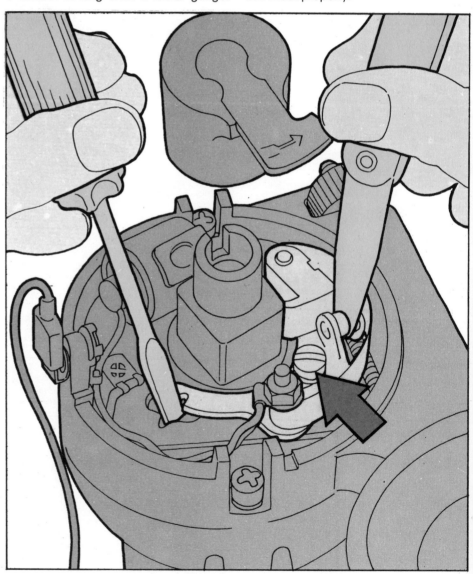

A sequence of photographs showing the adjustment procedure for the contact points of an Alfasud. The engine must first be turned so that the points are wide open (above left) and the gap checked (above right); if necessary, adjustment should then be carried out with a screwdriver and feeler gauge (below left). The fourth picture shows a bulb in use to check the exact moment when the contact points break

REPLACING THE POINTS

There are two types of contact set: the older, two-piece, variety and the modern one-piece 'Quickafit' version. The one-piece points are easier to fit than the older sort, but they can be less reliable. Removal and refitting of both types involves the unscrewing of the screw which holds the points down and fixes the adjustment. One nut holds the wires on and with the one-piece points the wires can be removed or fitted with points on or off.

The distributor has more functions than simply providing the basis for a spark. It decides when that spark should occur and at what point each cylinder should receive it (this is done by the rotor arm).

GENERAL MAINTENANCE

Basic ignition timing is simply a matter of distributor position rather than distributor function, but alteration of this setting with increasing engine speed is definitely a function of this complex instrument. Centrifugal weights are thrown outwards as speed of rotation rises and thus move the camshaft relative to its drive, within the distributor. It is possible for these weights to stick either 'advanced' or 'retarded', so oil should be applied sparingly down the centre of the distributor camshaft (the main spindle).

In addition to the centrifugal advance mechanism, there is usually a vacuum unit which alters the ignition timing with throttle opening by moving the contact points base plate (as depression increases the ignition is advanced). With the distributor cap removed, the tube leading to the distributor should be sucked. If the base-plate, which carries the contact set, moves, all is well, but if it does not and air is felt to be passing through the tube, then there is probably a leak, either in the diaphragm, or in the pipe.

The final job of the distributor is that from which the unit takes its name: distributing. The rotor arm fitted to the end of the shaft spins and passes high-tension current from a central contact in the distributor cap to several peripheral ones in turn (one for each cylinder). In fact the arm should not actually touch the peripheral ones — a spark jumps from its tip to each contact.

However, the central carbon contact is meant to touch the arm and is sprung for that purpose. Should the spring weaken or the carbon contact wear unduly, then the fault will need to be remedied. All the contacts should be cleaned regularly as should the rotor arm itself.

With all these simple procedures carried out every so often, ths distributor should present no problems.

IGNITION TIMING

There is no point in trying to adjust the ignition timing until the distributor has been correctly set up, as already detailed. With most distributors, for every variation of 0.001in in the setting of the contact-breaker points, there is a possibility of a three degree timing error. What is more, the biggest spark possible will be no good if it occurs at the wrong time or cylinder.

In most modern engines, the correct time is when the piston is about to reach the top of its compression stroke. A setting in advance of this will usually lead to 'pinking' (the name given to the tinkling noise caused by detonation of the mixture in the com-

bustion chamber), and a retarded setting will lead simply to a loss of efficiency. The reason that the spark plug fires before the piston is ready to move down on its power stroke is that the full effect of the spark is not immediately felt — it takes a few milliseconds for the mixture of fuel and air to combust.

Before attempting to set the timing, it is necessary to ascertain the position recommended by the manufacturer and especially to check whether this is a static setting (with the engine stationary) or a setting for so many rpm, in which case the automatic advance mechanisms may have taken over.

USING A BULB

Below right: a bulb is the most accurate indication of when the points open

Below: a cutaway view of a four-cylinder distributor, showing the major parts

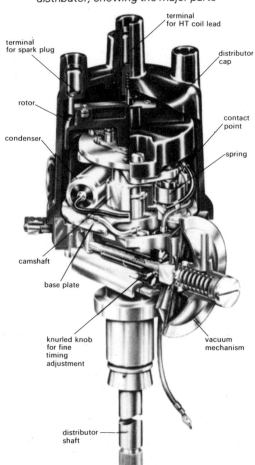

terminal for HT coil lead

terminal for spark plug

distributor cap

rotor

contact point

condenser

spring

camshaft

base plate

knurled knob for fine timing adjustment

vacuum mechanism

distributor shaft

Assuming a static figure is given, then the setting should be checked by connecting a small bulb to the contact breaker terminal on either the distributor or the high-tension coil and to earth (something like a cylinder block). This bulb should light up when the

ignition is on and the points are open — when they are shut the bulb will be short-circuited.

With the bulb connected, the engine should be turned until number one piston is approaching the top of its compression stroke. A mark on the

crankshaft pulley usually denotes 'top dead centre' as it is known when it coincides with a further mark on the timing cover. Also, there are usually degree marks on the timing cover to indicate how far before top dead center the crankshaft is. The engine should be turned by hand with the ignition on (perhaps by pushing in top gear) when approaching the relevant one of these marks. The light should just be coming on as this mark is reached. If it comes on before, the ignition is advanced and it comes on after, the ignition is retarded.

Most distributors have a knurled nut built in, with which it is possible to alter the ignition setting over a limited range, but if the setting is a long way out, it will be necessary to loosen the body of the distributor and turn it in the direction of shaft rotation to retard the setting and in the opposite direction for more advance. The distributor is held into its fixing bracket by a clamp bolt (like an exhaust clamp), so it is only necessary to loosen this one bolt in order to turn the mechanism.

FINE ADJUSTMENT

If an incorrect setting can be rectified by the use of the fine adjustment, all well and good (in most Lucas distributors there are eleven 'clicks' to one degree). However, should this system be unable to cope with the alteration, then the adjuster should be centred, *ie* the number of clicks from one end to the other should be counted and the nut left at a setting midway between the two.

With the clamp bolt loose, the distributor body should be turned and the setting checked in the same way as before. If it is nearly correct and a fine adjustment mechanism is fitted, then the clamp should be retightened and the final setting procedure left to this adjuster.

It should be noted that although most cars have their timing marks on the crankshaft pulley, as stated, some, notably the British Leyland Mini with

its transverse engine, have them on the flywheel (a plate has to be removed from the Mini's clutch housing in order to see the marks and even then a mirror is needed).

Right: the fine adjuster on a Lucas distributor; this should be centred before any major timing adjustments are carried out

USING A TIMING LIGHT

If the static setting is not known, or it is required to check the static setting in another way, then a stroboscopic timing light can be used. This type of light has a high-voltage 'bulb' which is connected to the spark plug lead on number one cylinder so that, every time the plug fires, the bulb lights up.

Right: a stroboscopic timing light in use on a 1700cc Morris Marina engine; it is essential to have dark surroundings in order for the procedure to work

By shining this light on to the timing marks, when the engine is running, the pulley should appear stationary and it should thus be possible to ascertain the setting of the ignition for any rpm.

In many engines, it will be necessary to remove the cooling fan in order to avoid the loss of a hand, so great care should be taken when experimenting. Also, there is no point in checking the ignition in this way if there is no means of knowing the speed of the engine. An accurate tachometer is needed for this.

Of course, there is no reason why the ignition setting should alter, unless the engine is dismantled, but it is often true that a garage will supposedly service a car and give it back to its owner with all sorts of incorrect settings, not least the ignition timing.

The main point to remember is that ignition timing should never be tackled without first correcting the contact-points gap.

CARBURETTOR ADJUSTMENT

The majority of carburettors will be one of two basic types: the fixed-venturi carburettor or the constant-vacuum carburettor. The fixed-venturi type may also be termed a fixed-jet or constant choke, and includes products of Solex, Zenith, Ford and Weber. Constant-vacuum types may be described as variable-jet or controlled-jet, and include those of SU and Stromberg manufacture.

Although the purpose of both types is the same, the construction and operation of each is entirely different, and the adjustment of the two types must be considered independently.

However, before carrying out any carburettor adjustments, check the ignition timing and examine the sparking plugs and points; reset or renew them as necessary. Having done this, inability to obtain a satisfactorily smooth-running engine may be due to burnt or badly seating valves. Equally likely is the possibility that an air leak is present in the inlet manifold or in the carburettor itself, thus weakening the mixture. Such an air leak could be caused by a faulty gasket or a worn throttle spindle.

FIXED-VENTURI CARBURETTORS

Fixed-venturi carburettors maintain a constant fuel/air ratio by means of three or more jets. Each of these jets contributes to the fuel/air ratio over part of the engine speed range.

A slow-running jet supplies fuel at small throttle openings, whereas at medium throttle openings, fuel is drawn in through a compensating jet. At large throttle openings and higher engine speeds, a main jet comes into operation.

A number of effects are utilised to control the time at which the various jets come into operation: the vacuum generated in the carburettor, the degree of throttle opening, and the tendency for the fuel level to decrease in certain parts of the carburettor as fuel consumption increases with engine speed.

Although the compensating and main jets are inoperative at low engine speeds, the slow-running jet is operative at all speeds. However, because of the relatively small quantity of fuel

Below: two types of Zenith fixed-venturi carburettor, both of the single-choke variety and possessing all the 'standard' features

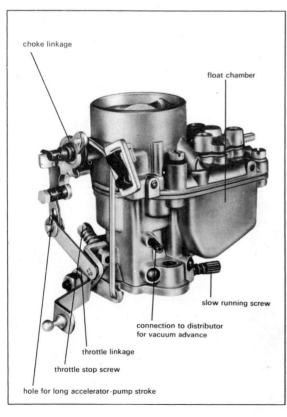

choke linkage

float chamber

slow running screw

connection to distributor for vacuum advance

throttle linkage

throttle stop screw

hole for long accelerator-pump stroke

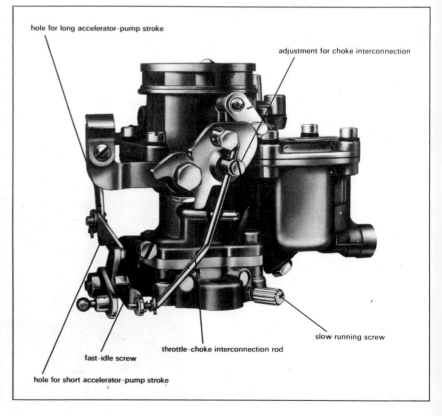

hole for long accelerator-pump stroke

adjustment for choke interconnection

slow running screw

throttle-choke interconnection rod

fast-idle screw

hole for short accelerator-pump stroke

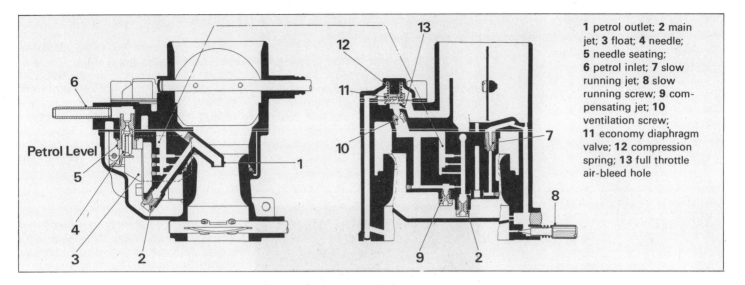

1 petrol outlet; 2 main jet; 3 float; 4 needle; 5 needle seating; 6 petrol inlet; 7 slow running jet; 8 slow running screw; 9 compensating jet; 10 ventilation screw; 11 economy diaphragm valve; 12 compression spring; 13 full throttle air-bleed hole

Above: sections through the Zenith series IV carburettor, as illustrated left on the opposite page; these show all the major components which may need to be removed or adjusted to retain maximum efficiency

Right: adjusting the slow-running mixture on a Weber double-venturi carburettor, again of the fixed-venturi type

supplied by the slow-running jet, adjustment of it will not appreciably effect the fuel/air ratio at medium and high engine speeds. Normally the slow running jet is the only jet which can be adjusted.

To set the slow-running adjustment, the engine must be at its normal operating temperature. Screw the throttle-stop screw in (clockwise) until the ignition warning light goes out completely. This will prevent the engine stalling when the mixture is being adjusted. Screw out (anticlockwise) the slow-running adjustment until the engine 'hunts' in a rhythmic manner. Screw in the slow-running adjustment until the hunting disappears and the engine runs smoothly.

Note that on some makes of fixed-venturi carburettor, the slow-running adjustment screw determines the mixture by regulating the air flow, and on others it regulates the fuel flow. Therefore, to achieve the same (say, weakening) effect, the screw may have to be unscrewed, or screwed in.

Reduce the engine speed to the normal tick over speed, with the ignition warning light flickering. If necessary, reset the slow-running adjustment as before.

Accelerator pumps on fixed-venturi carburettors are usually operated by a spring-loaded linkage from the throttle. Two settings may be provided on the linkage. The setting giving the shorter stroke is the summer setting, for warmer temperatures. The longer stroke is the winter setting, when the air temperature is lower and a richer mixture is required. In practice, many people do not pay any attention to this adjustment and the carburettor functions reasonably well with the accelerator pump linkage on the short stroke (summer setting), throughout the year.

The choke usually takes the form of a butterfly in the outer part of the carburettor barrel, which restricts the air flow to the engine.

The choke butterfly is connected to the throttle butterfly by an adjustable linkage, so as to provide a higher slow-running speed in cold conditions, to prevent stalling. The degree of throttle opening necessary will differ from one type of engine to another. To set this adjustment correctly, it will be necessary to resort to the car manufacturer's maintenance literature, or to set it by trial and error. To ensure accurate reassembly, if the carburettor is stripped for cleaning, this linkage should be marked in such a way that it may be reassembled to its original setting.

Fixed-venturi carburettors are quite simple to strip and clean, provided that a note is made of the correct position of each component as it is removed; additionally, ensure that the necessary renewable items are available, such as fibre-washers and gaskets, which can often be bought in service-kit form. Jets should be cleaned by blowing, or by using a jet of compressed air, in the opposite direction to the fuel flow (particularly with internally tapered jets, from the smaller aperture towards the larger aperture). Any attempt to clear jets with wire may result in the hole becoming enlarged, thus giving incorrect metering of the fuel supply.

Wash any sediment from the passageways in the body of the carburettor, and from the float chamber, with petrol, and blow them dry with compressed air. When reassembling the carburettor, use new gaskets and seals, but do not use any gasket sealing compound. Ensure that screws are tightened firmly and evenly, but without any undue force, as it is easy to strip threads, or distort parts of the carburettor body.

CONSTANT-VACUUM CARBURETTORS

Right: mixture adjustment on the HS series of SU constant-vacuum carburettors is simple, requiring only a spanner — or possibly just fingers — to turn the nut which moves the jet up or down

Below: a diagram of a similar carburettor, showing the major external components

1 jet adjusting nut; **2** jet locking nut; **3** dashpot; **4** fast-idle screw; **5** throttle stop screw; **6** fast-idle cam lever.

Constant-vacuum carburettors, such as the SU or Stromberg, maintain a constant fuel/air ratio by means of a single jet, within which a tapered needle is moved as the throttle is opened, in conjunction with a piston which controls the area of the venturi throat.

The needle and the piston are not linked to the throttle mechanically, but are lifted by the vacuum created in the the carburettor when the throttle is opened. The diameter and position of the needle, and the piston position ensure that the correct fuel/air ratio is obtained under all conditions.

On accelerating, the throttle is opened and the vacuum will raise both the needle and piston; an oil-controlled damping device causes this movement to be delayed, however, which reduces the size of the venturi and thus enriches the mixture.

Adjustment of the slow-running mixture on a constant-vacuum carburettor will affect the mixture supplied at high engine speeds and it is therefore important that the slow-running mixture is set correctly.

Before adjusting the slow-running mixture, check that the piston operates freely by lifting it and allowing it to fall. It should drop with a metallic click. Be very careful not to damage the sliding surface of the piston. If the piston sticks, loosen and reseat the dashpot cover; ensure that the dashpot cover screws are tightened evenly and replenish the dashpot oil to the correct level.

Run the engine until it reaches its normal operating temperature and screw in the throttle-stop screw, until the ignition warning goes out. Turn the adjusting nut or screw on the jet to obtain maximum engine speed. Turn it to move the jet upwards until the engine speed begins to fall, then turn it downwards just enough to regain maximum idling speed.

Check the adjustment by lifting the piston slightly; the engine speed should increase then fall again to the original speed. If the engine speed falls below the original speed, the mixture is too weak, and the adjusting nut must be turned downwards. If the engine speed does not fall to the original speed, the mixture is too rich, and the adjusting nut must be turned upwards. If necessary repeat the test, turning the adjusting nut, one flat at a time, until the adjustment is correct.

Constant-vacuum carburettors may be dismantled for cleaning, but care must be taken not to damage the piston or the needle. Before dismantling, mark the dashpot cover so that it may be refitted correctly.

If a rubber diaphragm is fitted, examine it for any damage or deterioration. If there is any sign of cracking or perishing, it must be renewed. If the needle is suspected of being bent, this may be confirmed by rolling it along a flat surface. Unfortunately, this check will only confirm that it is bent, not that it is straight, and it may be necessary to check it by the substitution of a known good one.

Clean the piston, and the dashpot interior, using petrol and a soft, clean cloth. Ensure that the cloth leaves no fluff because this may cause the piston to stick. The piston and the dashpot interior must never be cleaned with abrasives, neither should any attempt be made to remove any metal to prevent the piston sticking. If sticking occurs, it may be caused by damage to the piston or dashpot, incorrect orientation or bad seating of the dashpot in the carburettor.

MULTIPLE CARBURETTOR INSTALLATIONS

Multiple carburettor installations are adjusted for mixture strength and idling speed in much the same way as individual carburettors. However, it is essential that the throttles of individual carburettors on a multiple carburettor installation are synchronised.

Both types of carburettor may be synchronised by listening to the hiss, generated in each one, with a stetho-

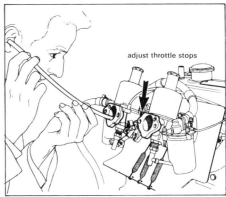

adjust throttle stops

scope or a piece of rubber tubing, and adjusting the throttle openings to obtain an equal 'hiss' from each one.

Fixed-venturi carburettors may also be synchronised by blanking off each one in turn, at tick over speed, and adjusting the throttles so that the reduction in engine speed is the same for each carburettor.

Oddly enough, synchronisation often proves to be a job for the specialist.

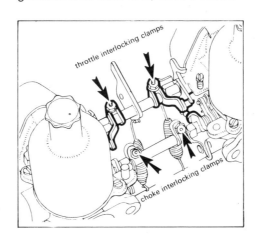

throttle interlocking clamps

choke interlocking clamps

Far right: a piece of rubber tube is an aid to balancing multiple carburettors; care must be taken to ensure that it is positioned identically in each carburettor mouth

Right: if adjustment is required, one of the interlocking clamps must be loosened and the throttles synchronised; the same applies if the chokes do not open simultaneously

FLOATS AND FLOAT CHAMBERS

The function of the float chamber is to maintain the correct level of fuel in the carburettor, so that there is sufficient for the engine requirements yet not so much that there is a risk of flooding.

The level of the fuel in the float chamber is maintained by a float and a needle valve. As fuel is used, the float falls and allows the needle valve to open, admitting more fuel. As the float chamber fills, the float rises and progressively closes the needle valve, maintaining the required fuel level.

Remove the float chamber cover and the float, and wash out any sediment with petrol; dry the components with a compressed air jet. Check that the float is not punctured by immersing it in a bowl or bucket of heated water; air bubbles from the float will indicate a puncture. Determine the effectiveness of the needle valve by blowing in the inlet and gently closing the needle valve with the finger. Reassemble the float chamber, fitting a new gasket.

The correct adjustment of the carburettor will ensure that the engine can develop maximum power with minimum cost and pollution. More apparent, however, will be the pleasant operation of the engine.

BATTERY

Right: batteries can be damaged in various ways; this photograph shows sulphation caused by lack of electrolyte and plates bent by overloading

Below: a cutaway view of a six-cell, 12-volt battery

Bottom: if the top of a battery is not kept clean, lead sulphate and lead oxide will be inclined to form

The lead-acid battery is used universally in the production car of 1980 It is heavy, due to the large amounts of lead, and it is not particularly efficient, but the alternatives are far more expensive or far less efficient.

The car battery has to be capable of supplying an enormous current (up to 300 amps) for the starter motor without sustaining any damage. If the engine is reluctant to start, the battery will be expected to provide plenty of tries before it runs flat. This requirement will not be achieved unless the unit is kept in good condition.

No battery will last for ever, although many are guaranteed for three years, but regular careful maintenance can prolong life well beyond this time. There are several reasons for the eventual failure of the lead-acid accumulator. The first is known as sulphation: as the battery discharges, a layer of lead sulphate is formed on the plates, which consist of lead and lead peroxide, and water is formed to dilute the sulphuric acid electrolyte; it is when this layer of sulphate becomes permanent that the battery is finished. The second reason for failure is that vibration can dislodge the lead and lead peroxide from the plates, allowing it to fall to the bottom of each cell (most accumulators in cars have six two-volt cells to give twelve volts). The third reason is that too heavy a discharge for too long a period will overheat the plates and can make them bend, touch and short circuit.

negative terminal

filler cap

bituminous material

conductor between cells

top covering

positive terminal

casing

plate connector

positive plate

negative plate

separator

TOPPING UP

Sulphation can be reduced to a minimum by keeping the battery topped up to the correct level, which is just above the top of the plates or a special mark, and by keeping it fully charged. Only distilled water should be used to supplement the electrolyte: ordinary water may carry chemicals which could interfere with the correct chemical reaction within each cell.

The only way to prevent the plates being shaken apart is to keep the battery firmly mounted. It would help to place some sort of padding between the unit and its mounting, but care would have to be taken to ensure that no acid contacted — and reacted with — the padding. The main thing is not to let the battery shake around in its compartment. The plates will only bend if the battery is either short circuited or exposed to a massive discharge. The starter should not be operated for more than four or five seconds at a time, with slightly longer between attempts.

A white deposit will often build up on the top of the battery, especially around the terminals. This should be wiped off and any residue neutralised with an alkali such as sodium bicarbonate or lime water (care should be taken to ensure that no alkali finds its way into any of the cells).

REPAIRS

If the deposit forms regularly and quickly, the battery casing should be checked for leaks. Any cracks, which may be discovered, can be sealed with special repair materials, available from most accessory shops. Should an appreciable amount of acid have leaked away, this must be replaced with acid of a similar specific gravity, measured on a hydrometer. It is possible, although difficult, to obtain supphuric acid for a battery from a service station. Otherwise it is worth trying a chemist or a chemical supplier.

Some cars have their batteries fitted either in the luggage compartment or in the passenger space. These positions are cooler than one under the bonnet, so less water is consumed and checks need to be less frequent.

If the battery is removed, care should be taken to refit it the correct way round. With the more common type of terminal, reversal is impossible due to the difference in sizes, but the flat type can easily be mixed up.

The engine and all the accessories (except the radio) will probably work quite well under these circumstances, but the dynamo will still be trying to charge 'the wrong way round', and this can do untold damage to the unit.

It is unwise to let a battery become totally flat, because of the problems with sulphation. However should it be too discharged to operate the self starter, it may be necessary to use an auxiliary charger. There is no need to remove the battery from the car, as long as all switches are in the off position. Before the charger is switched on, the electrolyte level should be correct and the top(s) removed to allow any gas to escape.

CHECKING SPECIFIC GRAVITY

Below: many modern batteries have a transparent or translucent casing, which facilitates checking of the electrolyte level, and most have an 'easy fill' arrangement, whereby all the cells may be filled at once after removal of a single cover

The best way to check the state of charge of a battery is to measure the specific gravity of the electrolyte in each cell. A flat cell will show a hydrometer reading of around 1.15 while a fully charged one should read between 1.28 and 1.3. If the battery, or just one of its cells, has ceased to function correctly, due to one of the reasons already given, the specific gravity of the acid will never rise above about 1.15, no matter how long the charger is connected.

If a hydrometer is not available, the battery should be charged until it has been 'gassing' for about two hours. The gases given off are hydrogen and oxygen, formed by the breakdown of some of the water in the electrolyte. This mixture is explosive, so naked lights should be kept well clear of the battery; an exploding car battery is extremely dangerous.

Several instrument manufacturers market gauges known as battery condition indicators. These are voltmeters with their scales marked to indicate, supposedly, the state of the battery's charge. However, even a malfunctioning battery may be able to produce a voltage of twelve or more when no current is being drawn, but this voltage will probably drop well below twelve as soon as the headlights are turned on. In other words, if the voltage remains at twelve or above, with the headlights switched on, then the battery is probably in good condition.

Off load, a cell in good condition should produce 2.15 volts, so a 'twelve-volt' battery will actually be a 12.9-volt one. During running, with the generator charging, the voltage should be around fifteen. Should a battery fail within its guarantee period, which may be one, two or three years, depending on the quality of the battery, it should be returned to the suppliers. Unfortunately, the manufacturers may only refund a percentage of the purchase price, related to the length of service the battery has given, but this is better than no guarantee at all.

STORAGE

Finally, if the car is going to be out of use for a long time, more than two or three months, it will be worthwhile to drain the electrolyte from the battery. First, the unit should be fully charged, then the sulphuric acid should be tipped out and stored carefully in a glass bottle, preferably with a ground-glass top (something which will not be attacked by the acid). It is advisable to rinse each cell out with distilled water, to remove all traces of the acid, and thus prevent any further chemical reaction within the battery.

In this way, the battery will remain 'dry charged' for an unlimited period. Replacement of the acid should render the battery ready for use once more, no further charging being necessary; the charge should not leak away in this state. When replacing the acid, take care that it is distributed evenly between the cells. No further acid should be added; use distilled water only.

WHEELS

To most people it seems that the only maintenance necessary on the wheels and tyres of a car is to check the air pressures inside the tyres, from time to time, and raise these pressures if necessary. It is usually left to a garage to decide when the tyres need replacing and to carry out that task at the right time

However, there is more to tyre and wheel maintenance than meets the eye, because neglect will often show no noticeable effects for many thousands of miles.

FITTING

When a wheel is fitted to a car, it is important to tighten the fixing nuts evenly to the correct torque. If the nuts are too tight, this may lead to stripped threads, to sheared studs or to the nuts being so tight that they cannot be undone.

If a wheel is changed by a garage or by a tyre-fitting specialist, its fixing nuts may well be tightened too much due to the fact that these concerns tend to use either large 'spider' wheelbraces, with great leverage, or pneumatic spanners, rather like electric drills in appearance.

It usually pays to spend five or ten minutes, after taking the car home, checking that the wheelnuts can be undone with the wheelbrace provided with the toolkit. If not, it is often possible to increase the leverage of

the brace by slipping a piece of piping over its free end. Failing this, the car should be returned to the company who fitted the wheels.

If centre-lock (knock-off) wheels are fitted, the central wheelnut will be one of two types: it may have two or three 'ears' on it, or it may be hexagonal. The eared type should be tightened or loosened by means of a soft-headed hammer — usually supplied with the car — using plenty of force when tightening. The hexagonal centre-lock nut is turned by means of a special ring spanner which is fitted to the nut and then hit with a hammer in the same way as is the eared nut.

Centre-lock wheelnuts are 'handed': those on the left-hand side of the car have a left-hand or unconventional thread, while those on the right-hand

Below right: the most popular type of wheel in current use, the steel disc variety with four-stud fixing

Below: a highly polished centre-lock wheel on a D-type Jaguar racing car. With disc wheels of this type, pegs locate each one on its hub while a central nut fixes it there

side have a right-hand or conventional thread. The purpose of this is that in this way the nuts will tend to tighten as the wheels propel the car forward. Obviously, it is impossible to fit a left-hand nut to the right-hand side — and *vice-versa*.

Drive is transmitted to centre-lock wheels, and from the wheels to the brakes, by means of splines or pegs, depending, often, on whether the wheels are spoked or of the disc type. It is not possible to fit a splined wheel incorrectly, but great care must be taken with a peg-driven wheel to make sure that the pegs are located in their holes, otherwise the pegs may be pushed out or the wheel may fall off.

SPOKED WHEELS

Right: in the early days of motoring (after artillery wheels had been ousted), centre-lock wire wheels were the most popular. More recently, however, they have been dethroned by the lighter and stronger steel or alloy equivalents

Spoked wheels need more attention than solid ones as it is important that the spokes are all kept at the correct tensions in order to prevent warping and buckling of the rims. Spoke adjustment is a job for an expert and should not be required very frequently as long as care is taken when driving.

BALANCING

Should a kerb be hit, this may well buckle the rim of a spoked wheel, this type being weaker than its disc cousin.

Right: with alloy wheels, such as this one on a racing car, balance weights have to be affixed by adhesive rather than clips, in order to avoid damaging chemical reactions

If any type of wheel suffers an impact it is likely to require rebalancing (imbalance can usually be felt as a shake in either the steering wheel or the whole car at a particular speed). Balancing is carried out on a special machine, weights being attached to the rim of the wheel to compensate for heavy portions opposite.

The balance weights are clipped to the rim of a steel wheel, but special weights, affixed by sticky tape, should be used on alloy wheels, which are susceptible to damaging chemical reactions between wheel and weight.

If a steel disc wheel is buckled, it should be discarded as it will be responsible for wheel vibration and inconsistent tracking.

TYRES

Modern tyres are very efficient and have long lives — especially radial-ply tyres, which last up to eighty per cent longer than cross-ply varieties and endow a car with greater cornering powers. Punctures, too, are less common now than in the early days of pneumatic tyres, due to the tougher nature of the compounds used in tyre manufacture.

PRESSURE CHECKS

A little care and attention, however, can lengthen the life of a tyre considerably. Apart from regular pressure checks and occasional inflation, most of the necessary attention is inherent in good, sensible driving.

RUNNING IN

Below: the results of various faults: heavy braking (1); misaligned wheel or suspension (2, 3, 4); over-inflation (5); under-inflation (6); worn wheel bearing and buckled wheel (7); imbalance and under-inflation (8)

Most parts of a car (those concerned with the going and stopping, anyway) require a certain 'running-in' period, during which those parts are not fully stressed and are given time, in effect, to get used to each other. The tyres are no exception; when they are new, they are smooth and shiny and are not particularly supple. If too much is asked of them too soon, in the way of fast cornering, hard acceleration or heavy braking, then they may overheat and suffer permanent damage. The strength in a tyre carcass is

1

2

3

4

5

6

7

8

provided by steel or textile bracing cords moulded into the rubber. As the tyre flexes under stress, friction will be responsible for the heat being generated in these cords. The newer the tyre, the greater this friction will be.

When a new tyre is fitted, its wheel should always be rebalanced. This is because there is always a slight imbalance built into a tyre and no two tyres are likely to be exactly the same — nor are they likely to be fitted the same way round on the wheel.

A badly balanced wheel will lead to rapid tyre wear and will often cause flats to appear on a tyre's cir-cumference. Imbalance can usually be felt however, as a vibration in the steering wheel (if the offender is a front wheel) or as a slight shake in the whole car.

Once a wheel has been balanced, it should stay balanced until its tyre is changed — unless, that is, it comes into violent contact with a kerb or with any other solid object which may upset the balance.

This type of impact can lead to alterations in various other suspension and steering settings which all manifest themselves in peculiar ways as far as tyre wear is concerned.

WEAR

The only reasons for a tread pattern are to disperse water and to ascertain the amount of wear; water is dispersed at a high rate through both longitudinal and lateral tread grooves

If the front-wheel toe-in is knocked away from its correct setting the front tyres will wear unevenly, as is shown in the pictures. Apart from the fact that one side of the tread may wear more quickly than the other, the edges of the tread will be 'feathered' — that is, one edge will have a rubber overhang.

This defect can be distinguished from an incorrect wheel-camber setting by the absence of feathering in the latter case. If the wheel is leaning too far to one side or the other, excessive wear will be experienced by one side of the tyre, although the tread blocks should still have sharp edges.

If a driver tends towards heavy braking, it is quite possible that flats will wear on some or all of the tyres. The chances are that this phenomenon will show itself more on the front tyres than on the rear, since most of the braking load is taken at the front.

If a brake is uneven, due to a warped drum or disc, or, perhaps, a bent drive shaft or stub axle, then the tyre fitted to the relevant wheel will tend to wear in the part which is touching the road when that brake 'grabs'. The answer here is to find whether the brake or the shaft is the faulty part and then either replace the shaft or have the drum or disc skimmed to give a flat surface.

A worn wheel bearing will also show itself in uneven tyre wear: as the wheel wobbles, the tyre load will be moved from one part of the tread to another and so worn spots will appear haphazardly on all parts of the tyre.

A buckled wheel will tend to wear one side of a tyre at one point on its circumference and another side at the opposite point. If this type of wear is apparent on a tyre it can only be caused by either a buckled wheel or a bent shaft (in the latter case brake grab would present itself as well).

Tyre pressures are not chosen arbitrarily; those recommended for a certain car are the ones which give optimum handling and road-holding, together with even tyre wear. An over-inflated tyre will wear the centre portion of its tread more than the outside edges, while one that is under-inflated will be inclined to the opposite. Under-inflation is usually shown up by tyre squeal under cornering, while over-inflation leads to a bumpy ride.

Every so often, a careful check should be made of all tyres, to make sure that they have no splits in them and that they are not bulging. It is important to check the inside walls, which cannot be seen easily.

Bulges can be caused by sharp objects penetrating the edge of the tread and allowing water to rot the cords. Any such sharp objects should be removed as soon as they are discovered and resultant punctures repaired by vulcanisation.

MAINTENANCE

This section explains how to carry out more complicated maintenance than normal servicing demands and also describes how common failures or wear and tear can be rectified. The fault-finding chart provides a simple guide to diagnosis and repair.

FAULT FINDING

ENGINE

Starter will not turn engine but headlights dim Battery flat · Corroded or loose connections · Starter jammed · Seized engine

Starter will not turn engine but headlights unaffected Defective starter solenoid, switch or motor · Starter gear not engaging (motor will be spinning fast)

Engine turns too slowly to start Battery flat · Corroded or loose connections · Defective starter motor · Oil in sump too thick · Partial seizure of engine

Engine turns normally but will not fire Defective ignition system: spark plugs · contact-breaker points · condenser · high-tension coil · rotor arm · distributor cap · leads and connections · Defective fuel system: fuel pump · carburettor · fuel lines · fuel tank (check fuel level and make sure air can enter at the top)

Engine backfires through exhaust pipe or carburettor, or kicks back Spark plug leads transposed · Ignition timing faulty · Valve timing faulty

Engine fires but will not run Defective fuel system, as above · Inconsistent spark (sporadic fault in ignition system)

Engine will not idle when cold Choke operation incorrect

Engine will not idle when hot Incorrect carburettor slow-running or mixture adjustment · blocked slow-running jet · choke stuck on · float chamber flooding · carburettor piston sticking (SU or Stromberg) or intake air leak

Engine idles roughly Carburettor mixture incorrectly adjusted · incorrect contact-breaker points gap · dirty or incorrectly set spark plugs · ignition timing faulty or intake air leak

Engine will not accelerate cleanly Carburettor faulty: accelerator pump · choke · mixture setting or · in SU or Stromberg seized piston or lack of

damper oil · Insufficient fuel supply · Dirty air cleaner · Short circuit inside distributor · Intake air leak

Engine loses power Accelerator adjustment incorrect · Insufficient compression · Ignition timing incorrect · Valve timing incorrect · Contact-breaker or sparkplug points gap incorrect · Valve clearances incorrect · Intake air leak · Partial seizure

Engine misfires or pulls back Ignition system faulty: check as for 'Engine turns normally but will not fire' · Dirty air cleaner · Contaminated fuel or low level

Engine runs on after switching off or 'pinks' Excessive carbon deposits in combustion chambers · Incorrect fuel grade · Incorrect spark plug type · Overheating

Engine overheats Lack of coolant · Faulty hose · Loose fan belt · Defective thermostat · Coolant passages blocked · Air passages through radiator blocked · Faulty cooling fan · Ignition timing incorrect · Carburettor mixture setting incorrect · Faulty cylinder head gasket · Faulty water pump

Excessive fuel consumption Incorrect carburettor mixture setting · Choke stuck on

Excessive oil consumption Worn piston rings, cylinders or valve guides · Oil leak

Oil warning light comes on at low speeds, or stays on all the time, or gauge reading low Low oil level · Faulty switch · Faulty gauge · Worn crankshaft bearings (usually accompanied by knocking noise) · Faulty oil pick-up pipe · Faulty oil pump

Oil warning light comes on or gauge reading falls during cornering or braking Low oil level · Faulty oil pick-up pipe

Ignition warning light stays on above tick-over, or ammeter shows discharge Broken or loose fan belt · Faulty generator · Faulty control box · Faulty wiring

TRANSMISSION

Car does not move when in gear with engine running Slipping clutch (if prop shaft not turning) · Gear not engaged properly or gearbox faulty (also if prop shaft not turning) · Broken prop shaft · Broken drive (half) shaft · Faulty final-drive unit · Hub slipping on shaft

Gears difficult to engage Clutch out of adjustment or faulty · Clutch hydraulic system faulty · Gearbox faulty · Lack of gearbox oil

Clutch slips Out of adjustment · Worn out · Greasy linings

Clutch judders Clutch internals off centre · Spring(s) broken · Worn engine or transmission mountings

Gears grate when changed Incorrect clutch adjustment · Faulty clutch · Worn synchromesh in gearbox

Slips out of gear Worn internal gearbox linkage

Gearbox noisy Low oil level · Wear

Clutch noisy when depressed Worn release bearing

BRAKES

Greater force than usual needed to operate brakes Damaged, worn or incorrect linings · Seized wheel-cylinder piston · Faulty servo (if fitted) · Overheated linings

Brakes stick on when pedal released Seized wheel-cylinder piston · Maladjustment of shoes · Broken or weak return springs · Seized handbrake

Brakes fierce Damaged discs or drums. Rust on discs or drums · Worn or damaged linings

Complete and sudden brake failure Broken hydraulic pipe · Failed hydraulic cylinder · Low fluid · Broken pedal link

Brakes judder Brake component at wheel not firmly mounted · Faulty disc or drum · Worn or damaged linings

Excess pedal travel Brake shoes maladjusted · Air in hydraulic system · Maladjustment between pedal and master cylinder

Pedal not firm (spongy) or needs pumping Air in hydraulic system · Fault in master cylinder · Hydraulic fluid leak

Car pulls to one side under braking Damaged or worn brake linings on one side · Seized piston in wheel cylinder on one side · Maladjustment of brakes on one side · One under-inflated tyre

SUSPENSION

Soft and bouncy ride Failed dampers · Broken spring · Broken damper mounting · Tyre pressure too low

Hard ride Seized suspension joint · Stiff or seized damper · Broken spring (causing suspension to hit stops) · Tyre pressure too high

Car handles badly Failed dampers · Failed wheel bearing · Flat tyre · Failed suspension component · Loose wheel

Car rolls excessively Failed damper · Broken damper mounting · Weak or broken spring · Broken or disconnected anti-roll bar

Nose drops excessively under braking Failed front dampers · Broken damper mountings · Weak or broken front springs

Rear drops excessively under acceleration Failed rear dampers · Broken damper mountings · Weak or broken rear springs

Knocking felt through steering or body, especially when passing over bumps Worn suspension bushes · Weak springs or failed dampers allowing bottoming · Loose wheel · Loose suspension component · Failed wheel bearing

STEERING

Car handles badly or wanders Loose wheel · Flat tyre · Incorrect steering alignment · Failed components

Car pulls to one side Incorrect tyre pressure one side · Unmatched tyres · Incorrect alignment · Brakes binding

Steering or whole car vibrates when travelling, even with engine off Wheel(s) out of balance (usually felt through steering) · Wheel(s) buckled or loosely fitted · Tyre(s) damaged · Universal joint(s) on prop shaft or drive shaft(s) worn out · Wheel bearing failed

FAULT RECTIFICATION

ENGINE

Below: if the starter cannot be freed by rocking the car, a spanner must be employed to turn the squared shaft

Above right: if a fuel system defect is suspected, check that fuel is reaching the carburettor by removing the pipe from the float chamber

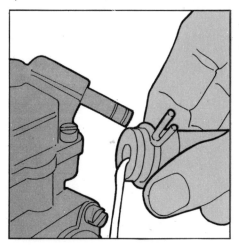

Flat battery Push or tow-start the car, but check that there is no discharge when everything is turned off, either with an ammeter or by looking for sparks on disconnecting or reconnecting the main battery lead. If, after charging, the battery soon runs down, even though it is correctly topped-up, it must be renewed.

Starter jammed Engage top gear and remove the handbrake; rock the car backwards and forwards until the starter disengages. If this fails, turn the squared end of the starter shaft with a spanner.

Seized or partially seized engine The unit should be stripped to find the cause; this is a skilled job and is best left to a trained mechanic.

Defective starter solenoid or switch These items should be replaced if the starter works when either is bypassed.

Starter gear not engaging If the starter is of the older inertia type, then it must be removed and the bendix gear freed by cleaning with petrol; if it is of the newer pre-engaging type, then the solenoid must be checked and, if necessary, replaced.

Defective ignition system Remove a spark plug lead from its plug cap hold its end close to the cylinder head and look for a spark when the engine is turned with the ignition on. Alternatively, if you have a spare spark plug, connect one of the leads to this and hold it against the engine. If there is a spark, then the spark plugs must be cleaned or replaced. If there is no spark, the distributor points should be cleaned and adjusted, but if this does no good and the leads and connectors are okay, then there may be a fault in the distributor cap (check that the central carbon brush is protruding far enough to touch the rotor arm) or rotor arm (it may have twisted on its shaft). It is very rare for the condenser to break down, but it can be disconnected temporarily. If all else fails, the high-tension coil must be checked, but the problem usually lies with the distributor, leads, or plugs.

Defective fuel system First check that fuel is reaching the carburettor, by removing the pipe from the float chamber and turning the ignition on (electric pump) or turning the engine over (mechanical pump). If no fuel pours out of the pipe, then the fuel pump is probably faulty, although there may be a blockage in the pipe or the fuel-tank vent. *Make sure there is fuel in the tank.* The diaphragm of a mechanical pump can be replaced quite easily and cheaply, but spares for electric pumps are not so easy to come by, so it is common to fit a replacement unit. If everything is working here, and fuel is coming out, then the fault probably lies in the carburettor itself. Make sure fuel is entering the float chamber and is filling it to the correct level; also clean all the jets, without disturbing settings.

Ignition timing or valve timing faulty These should be checked and adjusted as shown in the sections on pages 22-3.

Inconsistent spark This can be caused by any of the faults listed under 'Defective ignition system'.

Incorrect carburettor adjustment The settings should be checked following the instructions on pages 24-7.

Float chamber flooding The fuel level should be altered by adjusting the float valve or, if the valve is worn, the assembly should be replaced.

Carburettor piston sticking This only applies to SU or Stromberg instruments and could be due to two faults. The first is a decentralised main jet, which can be cured by adjustment; the second is corrosion on the piston or cylinder, which can be rectified by cleaning both surfaces.

Intake air leak This is usually caused by a faulty gasket or a loose mounting. All nuts and bolts should be checked and any faulty gaskets replaced.

Valve clearances incorrect With a pushrod-and-rocker set-up, the clearances can be adjusted by means of a spanner, a screwdriver and a feeler gauge, or a special tappet-adjusting tool. The rocker cover should be removed so that the clearances between rocker and valve stem can be checked. If they are incorrect, the

locknuts must be loosened and the screw-adjusters turned until the correct setting is obtained. The locknut must then be tightened. Overhead camshafts usually require the use of shims (spacers) to give the required clearance, and the maker's literature should be consulted.

Carbon deposits in combustion chambers The cylinder head should be removed and the deposits scraped from the chambers and piston crowns, using a blunt instrument. At the same time the valves should be ground on to their seats, using a special tool and grinding paste — remember to re-adjust the valve clearances. See pages 44-6.

Loose fan belt This is usually adjusted by loosening the generator mounting bolts and moving that component until the play in the belt, on its longest run, is half an inch; if the belt is too tight damage to bearings can result.

Defective thermostat This item can be checked by removing it and placing it in boiling water. If it opens and closes, when hot and cold respectively, then it is functioning correctly.

Defective water pump The unit must be replaced, if it is defective, as it is not practicable to repair the pump. On most engines, this involves no more than removing the fan belt and fan, unbolting the unit and fitting the new one — with a new gasket.

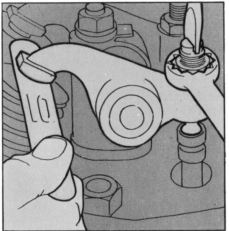

Right: in most pushrod engines, the valve clearances can be adjusted by means of a spanner, a screwdriver and a feeler gauge in the manner shown here

Below: the fan belt is usually adjusted by loosening two or three nuts and pulling the dynamo or alternator back

Below right: if a faulty thermostat is suspected, it should be removed and placed in boiling water to check whether it opens

Defective oil switch or gauge
Switches are fairly cheap, but gauges should be repaired by their manufacturers.

Worn crankshaft bearings In most cases, if the crankshaft bearings are worn, the shaft itself will be damaged and will have to be reground by a specialist before new bearings are fitted.

Defective oil pick-up pipe Unfortunately, major dismantling is required to reach this pipe — probably a job for a garage as the engine may have to be removed from the car.

Defective generator Alternators and dynamos both need new brushes every so often. These are cheap and can be fitted by removing the end cover from the generator.

Both alternators and dynamos have brushes to transmit current to or from their rotating elements. In an alternator (near right), it is usually possible to gain access to the brushes simply by removing a dust cover, while a dynamo (far right) will usually have to be taken off the engine and its end cover removed

---

TRANSMISSION

Gears not engaging properly This may mean that the gearbox itself is worn (which will necessitate a major overhaul — it is often cheaper to fit a replacement box). Some cars, however, have adjustment provided in the linkage between the gear lever and the box itself. Even if there is no adjustment here the fault may lie in these parts — perhaps a bush is worn or a rod bent.

Faulty final-drive unit If the drive has completely disengaged, the chances are that a gear has stripped its teeth. It is possible to overhaul the unit, but it is easier to fit a replacement part — following the manufacturer's instructions.

Hub slipping on drive shaft This is a very unusual fault and can only happen if the Woodruff key, which is supposed to prevent this, has broken. The remedy is to remove the hub (a special extractor may be needed) get rid of any traces of the broken key and, assuming no further damage has been done, fit, a new part. On some cars, splines are used instead of a key and if these have stopped functioning, the shaft or hub or both must be replaced.

Clutch out of adjustment The manufacturer's literature should be consulted to find out whether or not your car has any clutch adjustment provided and, if so, what the correct setting should be. The clutch pedal should always have a small amount of free play, otherwise the release bearing — or the driven plate — will wear rapidly.

Clutch faulty If the gears are difficult to engage, then the clutch release bearing may be worn or broken. Alternatively, mechanical linkage from the hydraulic cylinder or cable may be damaged.

Clutch hydraulic system faulty If hydraulic fluid is not leaking out, then the fault is likely to be in the master cylinder, operated by the clutch pedal. The seals will probably be worn, so these should be replaced, making sure

There are two common ways of transmitting motion from drive shaft to hub: the most common is by way of a taper and Woodruff key (below) while some cars make use of splines (below right)

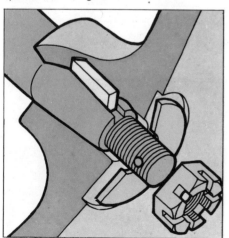 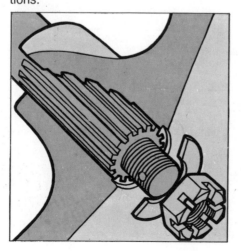

Right: the components of a typical diaphragm-spring clutch, which are, from the right, operating linkage (yellow), release bearing (red), pressure plate assembly, with diaphragm spring (blue) and driven plate (mustard)

that the cylinder itself is not damaged. Kits of seals can be bought for a small amount of money.

If fluid is leaking out, then either the pipe is damaged or loose, or the slave cylinder, which actually operates the clutch, is faulty. The procedure here is as for the master cylinder — in fact, if one cylinder is being overhauled, then it is also advisable to do the other. After such tasks have been completed, the hydraulic system must be bled. A bleed nipple will be provided on the slave cylinder and a tube should be fitted to this and dipped into a jar of clean fluid. The nipple should then be loosened a little and the pedal pumped until no further bubbles emerge into the fluid. The pedal must be held down while the nipple is tightened and then the reservoir in the master cylinder must be topped up.

Clutch worn out Any part of the clutch can become useless through wear, but the most common is the driven plate (this is the friction disc which sticks the engine to the gearbox). If a car has done many thousands of miles, then the springs which make the clutch work may well be weakened, so if the driven plate is being replaced the cover assembly, which incorporates the springs, is worth attention.

Greasy clutch linings If oil or grease have impregnated the linings, then the only real solution is to fit a new driven plate. The main thing, however, is to ascertain where the oil has come from — the chances are that either the crankshaft rear oil seal or the gearbox mainshaft front oil seal have failed. Replacing these is likely to require dismantling of the gearbox or removal of the sump.

Clutch internals off centre This usually means that the clutch cover assembly, and probably the driven plate too, will have to be replaced.

Worn engine or gearbox mountings The engine and gearbox are mounted on rubber, which stretches and perishes with age. Usually, wear will be obvious because the mountings will sag, but this is not always so and it may be worth renewing the mountings anyway.

Worn universal joints These can be replaced fairly easily, but the relevant shaft must be removed in order to carry out the job. See pages 47-8.

Worn synchromesh New synchromesh parts can be fitted, but this requires a major strip-down and the workshop manual for the car should be consulted.

General gearbox wear It is probably easiest and quickest to replace the whole gearbox, once it reaches this stage, since new gears, shafts, bearings etc will be expensive and fitting them will require a great deal of labour.

BRAKES

Brake component at wheel not firmly mounted In the case of drums, this may be the back plate, the cylinder(s), the shoes themselves or the pivot opposite the cylinder. Discs are simpler and the chances are that it will be either the caliper or the disc which has come loose.

Faulty disc or drum The most common fault in this area is that of scoring: if worn linings have been left in, metal will have touched metal, thus cutting grooves in the disc or drum. Sometimes, however, overheating may cause distortion of either of these

Right: if the brake pads are allowed to wear down to the metal backing section then the disc itself will become scored

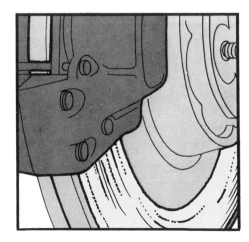

parts, so that the braking will be very jerky. In both cases, if the damage is not too severe, skimming is adequate.

Worn or damaged linings It is possible to buy brake-shoe linings to fit at home, but this is not worthwhile; it is far better to buy exchange shoes. Disc pads must be replaced as a whole, it is not feasible to reline them. They are not sold on an exchange basis, since there is so little metal involved and this is the only part which can be reclaimed.

Brake shoes maladjusted Check whether the brakes on your car are of the adjustable type, then jack up each wheel in turn, tightening the adjuster(s) until the brakes just bind.

Air in hydraulic system This usually leads to a spongy feel at the pedal. Each brake should be bled individually, starting with the one farthest from the master cylinder and ending with the nearest. See page 49.

Maladjustment between pedal and master cylinder It is very rare for this kind of adjustment to be provided, so, unless anything is worn or broken, the fault is likely to be in this area.

Fault in master cylinder The most common fault in a master cylinder is wear in the rubber piston seals. These can be replaced cheaply by removing the cylinder and stripping it down. See page 50.

Faulty servo Unless the fault is in the pipe which links the servo to the inlet manifold, in which case this can be replaced, it is wise to have the servo checked by an expert.

Overheated linings This phenomenon is known as fade and is very rare in disc brakes, although, even in modern types, drums can be affected. Fade is caused by unequal expansion of drum and shoes giving rise to reduced contact areas. The only cure is to stop and let the brakes cool down for a few minutes.

Seized wheel-cylinder piston Wheel cylinders should have covers to prevent dust and moisture creeping between the piston and cylinder. However, these covers perish with age and this can lead to rust forming on both piston and cylinder. If enough rust builds up, the piston may stick (usually in the on position). The remedy is to remove the offending piston(s) and remove all traces of rust, using metal polish if necessary. If you do use metal polish, make sure that all traces of it are removed before reassembly. If pitting is present in the surface which slides past the fluid seal, then a new piston or cylinder must be fitted. See page 51.

Broken or weak return springs This only applies to drum brakes. Both faults are extremely rare; a broken spring is obvious, but a weak one can only be spotted by comparing its length with that of a new spring.

Seized handbrake linkage If all pivots are lubricated regularly, this problem should not arise. However, if seizure does occur, the answer is to 'work' the pivots until they are completely free. Penetrating oil is a help here, but once the joints are released, ordinary lubricating oil or grease should be applied.

Rust on discs or drums This builds up very quickly, especially in damp weather, and it is easily dealt with by applying the brakes several times, fairly gently.

Broken hydraulic pipe This is an easy fault to find, as there will be a pool of fluid under the car, near the broken pipe. Replace the offending part and then bleed the brakes (see page 49). It is worth checking all the flexible pipes, from time to time, to make sure that they are not rubbing against anything and are not perished.

Failed wheel cylinder Once again, fluid will be evident, either on the ground, or around the faulty cylinder, should one of these have failed. As with the master cylinder, the cure is to remove the cylinder, take out the piston(s) and replace the rubber seals. In disc-brake cylinders, the seal is often found in the cylinder rather than on the piston. See pages 50-51.

SUSPENSION

Failed dampers It is not possible to dismantle telescopic dampers, but lever-arm dampers come apart and can be repaired. In fact the fault may simply be a lack of hydraulic fluid (this is special damper fluid and can be obtained from most accessory shops). If your car has MacPherson struts or Chapman struts (found only in Lotus models), you should be able to buy a damper insert kit, this saves replacing the whole strut, which is very expensive. See pages 52-3.

Seized suspension joint This is a rare fault, but it may occur, usually being caused by lack of lubrication and consequent rust. Brute force and penetrating oil is the answer here. Make sure plenty of grease is applied, once the joint is free (assuming it is not a rubber-bushed joint).

Stiff or seized damper Again, a very unusual fault, which normally requires replacement of a telescopic damper or repair of a lever-arm one. See page 53.

Failed wheel bearing Specialist tools may be required, in order to replace a wheel bearing. First the hub must be removed, then the bearing extracted — in some cases, the drive shaft must also be removed.

Failed suspension component Whichever part has gone wrong, the remedy is replacement, unless welding can be carried out. It may be just as cheap to replace the part.

STEERING

Loose wheel Obviously it is important to make sure that the wheels are not falling off, but be careful not to overtighten them; this may lead to the threads stripping or the studs shearing. Knock-off (centre-lock) wheels should be tightened with a soft hammer until the nuts will not turn any more. Knock-off wheels are 'handed' to prevent their undoing through the car's motion, so brute force is not needed.

Brakes binding Most drum brakes require occasional adjustment, although the latest types are self adjusting. If your brakes are of the type that do require attention in this way, then they should be tightened up, with the wheel off the ground and the handbrake off (for the relevant end of the car), until they are just beginning to bind. Noticeable binding, when the car is in use, may be caused by overenthusiastic adjustment or by either the mechanical or hydraulic parts sticking. In the case of disc brakes, any binding can only be caused by this sticking, as all discs are self adjusting. See pages 50 and 51.

Incorrect steering alignment A special tracking gauge is needed to rectify this fault, but a sure sign of maladjusted steering is a feathering of one side of every tread block on the front tyres. If a tracking gauge is available, the most usual method of adjustment is by loosening the lock-nut on one of the track rod ends and screwing the rod in or out of the end until the correct setting is achieved.

Tracking gauges are commonly available now and simple to use; the car is driven slowly over the gauge and the pointer indicates the degree of misalignment.

Play in steering or suspension It is sometimes possible to take up any play by adjustment, but it is more usual to replace the offending parts (with older steering boxes adjustment is provided, but removal of play in the straight-ahead position can lead to stiffness on lock). Suspension play is usually cured by the fitting of new rubber or metal bushes, whereas play in a track rod end will require replacement of that part — and subsequently re-alignment of the steering.

Unmatched tyres It is illegal in Britain to mix radial tyres on the front with cross-ply tyres on the rear, or to mix radial and cross-ply tyres on the same axle. Neither is it advisable to mix different makes of tyre on the same axle (sizes are sometimes slightly different, bracing materials vary and rubber mixes — not to mention tread patterns — are far from standard).

The most common method of adjusting steering alignment is to loosen the locking nuts on both track rods and screw in or unscrew both rods by equal amounts until the setting is correct; the lock nuts should then be securely tightened

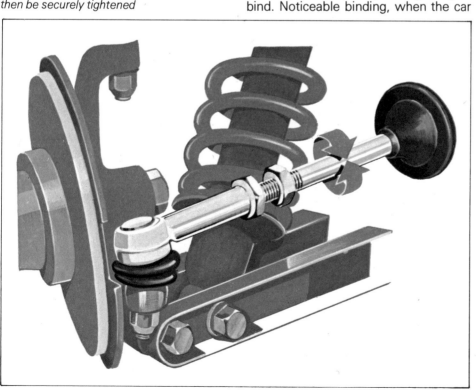

DECARBONISING

Any engine which runs on a hydrocarbon fuel is likely to suffer from a build-up of carbon deposits. Whether that engine be conventional petrol or diesel, rotary or even gas turbine, the same principle applies, but for the time being we will confine ourselves to reciprocating petrol engines.

EFFICIENCY REDUCED

There are three main reasons why carbon deposits are unwanted : gas flow is slowed down, combustion chamber size is decreased and 'hot spots' may be formed.

The basic governing factor for the efficiency of this type of engine is the rate at which the fuel/air mixture can enter each cylinder and the rate at which exhaust gases can leave. Smooth-sided passages are better than rough-sided ones, since the latter cause excessive turbulence and restrict the gas flow. Carbon deposits are, by nature, rough and therefore impair this efficiency.

A moderately tuned engine may not suffer by having its compression ratio raised, which is what happens as the combustion chamber size decreases, but others may begin to 'pink' (a tinkling noise caused by pre-ignition).

Pre-ignition is not always due to an over-high compression ratio, it may be caused by a 'hot spot'. The heat-conducting properties of carbon are not nearly as good as those of cast-iron or aluminium alloy, so heat built up by combustion can be stored in the layer of carbon, eventually reaching red heat and causing fuel to ignite while the piston is still approaching the top of its stroke.

One of the most common symptoms of excessive carbonisation is 'running-on' (the engine continues to run for some seconds after the ignition has been switched off). If either this phenomenon or 'pinking' is present in a petrol engine, and the recommended grade of fuel is being used, excessive carbon build up must be suspected.

SOLVENTS

The only really effective way of decarbonising an engine is to take off the cylinder head and scrape the various parts free of this element. There are 'decarbonising agents' on the market which can be introduced to the combustion spaces via the spark-plug holes. Leaving these solvents in for several hours is supposed to free the engine of its deposits, but unfortunately they remove nothing apart from a thin surface coating.

REMOVING THE CYLINDER HEAD

In any engine other than an overhead-camshaft power unit, removal of the cylinder head is a straightforward job requiring only the disconnection of ancillaries such as the exhaust pipe, coolant pipes, fuel pipe(s), wires and control cables and the disengagement of several fixing bolts or nuts. The carburettor(s) can often be left undisturbed, although, if the decarbonisation process is to be carried out properly, it or they should be removed at some stage to give access to the induction ports.

Of course, should the engine have side valves, it is quite possible that nothing other than the cylinder-head fixings need be undone — the inlet and exhaust will remain on the engine. However, it may still be desirable to take off at least the induction manifold, to avoid foreign bodies entering it and thence the carburettor(s), but, ideally, both manifolds.

OVERHEAD CAMSHAFTS

Overhead camshafts present a slightly greater problem, in that the drive to the shafts, and sometimes the shafts themselves, have to be removed. In fact, refitting of the shafts involves far more work than does removal, since the valve timing has to be adjusted. Great care should be taken when refitting a camshaft, to make sure that none of the valves hits a piston; the safest avoiding action is to set the crankshaft so that all the pistons are below the tops of their strokes and then the camshaft bearings can be refitted and tightened down to the correct torque.

REMOVING VALVES

If the job is to be carried out properly, the valves must all be removed and kept so that they can be replaced in their original seats. Probably the easiest way of remembering the order is to place all the valve stems, in order, through holes in a piece of card, numbering each hole accordingly.

A side-valve engine usually has a plate bolted to the side of the cylinder block to give access to the valve fixings and valve springs. If the valves are to be removed from an overhead-camshaft engine, the shaft or shafts will have to be removed before the valve-spring compressor is brought into play. With overhead valves and a block-mounted camshaft, the rocker shaft will have to be unbolted in order to clear the way for valve removal.

COMBUSTION CHAMBERS

Once the valves are out and marked, the process of decarbonisation can be started. A rotary wire brush, fitted to an electric drill, is very useful for cleaning the combustion chambers — from which the spark plugs should have been removed — but stubborn particles should be scraped off, using wood if possible, but soft metal if necessary, taking great care.

VALVE THROATS AND PORTS

The rotary brush can be used to clean out the valve throats and the ports (assuming the manifolds have been removed). The valves themselves can be cleaned by placing them in the chuck of the electric drill and using a scraper to clean the carbon from the head. Care should be exercised here, as it is essential to avoid damaging the valve seat and the stem where it passes through the guide in the cylinder head. Once the major part of the deposit has been removed, the valve can be polished with wet-or-dry paper.

Polishing is not essential for any of the parts, but it will take longer for carbon to build-up on a smooth, shiny surface, with few imperfections, than on a dull surface with many pits and bumps. Unfortunately, this build-up cannot be avoided, but its delay can only increase efficiency, for the reasons mentioned earlier.

Right: it may be necessary to scrape carbon from the valve stems and heads using a knife, but it is far easier to fit the valve into the chuck of an electric drill and hold a scraper against the valve while it rotates

Below right: an electric drill and a suitably sized rotary wire brush are ideal for cleaning out the valve throats and ports

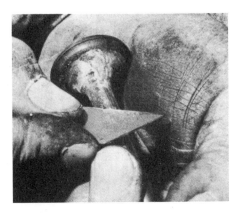

GRINDING THE VALVES

The valves should be ground to fit their seats, by resting them in place, with a little grinding paste between the contact surfaces, and twisting them to and fro with either a special suction tool or, in the case of grooved valve heads, a

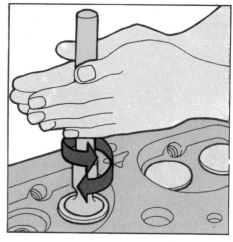

Before grinding in each valve, place some grinding paste around its seating surface (near right), then swivel it back and forth on its seat using a special tool and the method shown (far right)

screwdriver. When the seats are an even matt grey, with no pits, the grinding paste should be removed, the stem oiled and the springs and fixing devices replaced. If oil seals are used on the valve stems, new ones should be obtained in order to keep oil consumption to a minimum.

PISTONS

The carbon should be scraped from each piston crown, once again with wood if possible. It is advisable to leave a small ring of carbon around the edge of each piston (about 3/16in), so that any deposits in the space between the top piston rings and the crowns will not be disturbed and perhaps increase oil consumption.

As each piston is tackled, it should be placed at the top of its stroke and a piece of cloth used to cover the other cylinders and any oil passages. Loose carbon should be wiped away carefully.

REPLACING THE CYLINDER HEAD

Before replacing the cylinder head, its face and that of the block should be wiped and lightly greased to prevent the gasket sticking. A new gasket should always be used as the old one will have been flattened.

It is advisable to measure the tension of the nuts and bolts with a torque wrench, as uneven settings can lead to warping of the head and consequent leakage of compression, coolant or both.

Finally, valve clearances must be adjusted, as grinding the valve seats closes these up and too tight a setting may eventually lead to a burnt valve.

MANIFOLDS

Before refitting the inlet and exhaust manifolds (if these have been removed), any heavy deposits should be dispersed as much as possible. It is unlikely that any carbon will have found its way into the inlet pipes; if there is any, it may well indicate that the valve timing has been incorrectly adjusted (this should be obvious from the resultant poor running).

Any thick lumps of carbon should be scraped from the exhaust-manifold ends, to aid gas flow, although the high pressure in the exhaust system means that this is not essential.

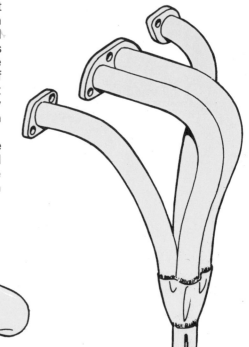

Right: two different types of exhaust manifold are common on production cars. These are the cast type (near right) and the fabricated tubular type, which is generally the more efficient

UNIVERSAL JOINT REPLACEMENT

There are several types of universal joint in use on modern cars, the most common being the Hooke joint used on many drive and propeller shafts.

The Hooke joint consists of a four-legged 'spider', which links the two forked ends of the shaft parts. Friction between the components is reduced by fitting roller bearings between the forks and the legs of the spider.

Some of these joints are fitted with grease nipples, so that the rollers can be lubricated, but those without nipples may run dry, despite the presence of rubber seals, and wear out.

Wear is indicated either by a clonk when the accelerator is depressed or released in gear, especially a low gear, or by a regular knocking when the car is moving.

Below: a selection of drive shafts and propeller shafts, with various types of universal joints; those encased in rubber 'boots' are of the constant velocity type, generally used on front-wheel-drive care

REPLACING A HOOKE JOINT

In order to replace a Hooke joint (repair, as such, is not possible), a kit should first be obtained from an accessory shop or motor-spares agent. The kit will contain a new spider, four new caps, containing roller bearings, and new circlips to retain the caps in the yokes. It is important to know the size of the joint fitted, as more than one is available — most cars use the smaller of two common sizes.

It is not easy to remove the old joint with the shaft in situ, as the task involves extracting the old caps and pressing in the new. However, it is often easy to remove the shaft to which the joint is fitted: at least one pair of yokes is usually bolted, by a flange, to its shaft.

With the shaft out of the car, the retaining circlips should be removed from grooves in each yoke, using either special circlip pliers or, perhaps, a pair of bradawls. Next, one half of the shaft should be rested on something solid such as a vice, while the other half is banged, in order to use the spider to force one cap partially out. When the shoulders of the spider are resting on the edges of the yoke,

the shaft should be turned through 180° and the procedure repeated with the cap on the opposite side. It should now be possible to remove the spider from these two caps and with this done the caps can be knocked out.

The same principle applies to the remaining pair of caps, but the spider itself, rather than the shaft (because the shaft has been removed), will have to be hammered.

The new spider can now be inserted between one pair of yokes and the bearing caps pressed in with a vice, making sure that the needle rollers are all upright and greasy, and that the rubber seals are fitted evenly. In the absence of a vice, a hammer can be used (with a wood block to avoid damage to the caps). It is necessary only to press the caps in far enough to allow the circlips to be fitted; any further movement will lead to stiffness in the joint.

The second pair of caps should be fitted in exactly the same way as the first. An important point is to make sure that the grease nipple, if one is fitted, faces in such a direction that it cannot impede flexure of the joint.

Below: components of the Hooke type of joint

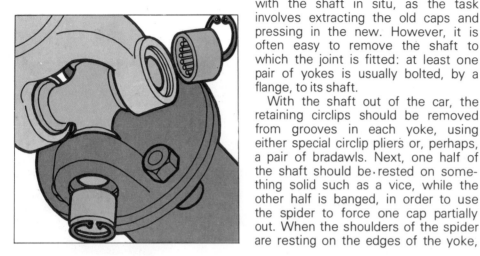

MINIS

Above: a rubber variety of Hooke joint

A type of Hooke joint is used on the BLMC Mini: early cars made use of a rubber-covered steel spider fixed to each part of the drive shaft by 'U' bolts; later cars had standard, though large-diameter, joints, with rollers, still retained by 'U' bolts.

It is very easy to replace either type of joint, as the shafts do not have to be removed due, in turn, to the caps being bolted on rather than pressed in,

a much simpler procedure.

The outer end of the Mini driveshaft, in common with other front-wheel-drive cars, uses a constant-velocity joint. This is more complicated than the Hooke-type and cannot be dismantled, having to be replaced as a whole. The standard symptom of wear is a loud knocking from the joint when the steering is turned hard over to one side.

REPLACING RUBBER 'DOUGHNUTS'

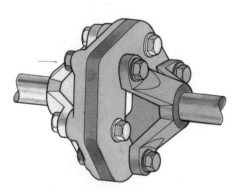

Above: a rubber 'doughnut'; the bend around the rubber section should be removed after the joint has been assembled

A third type of universal joint is the rubber 'doughnut', used on such cars as the Hillman Imp and the Lotus Elan. This consists of a rubber ring with an outside diameter of about five inches. The ring is hexagonal and carries six metal-lined bolt holes, one at each angle. The drive-shaft ends carry three pronged forks, each prong also carrying a hole. Bolts through these three holes pass through alternate holes in the 'Rotoflex' coupling, as it is known. The vacant holes are then filled by bolts, projecting from the other, similar, part of the drive shaft, nuts being placed on their ends.

When the assembly is complete, drive is transmitted through the flexible rubber between each pair of bolts. Eventually this rubber perishes and

splits, and replacement is necessary.

A special tool is available, which passes round the outside of the coupling and compresses the springy rubber, making it easy to remove the bolts. However, it is possible to use a large worm-drive clip, available from most accessory shops. With a compressor applied, the bolts, once the nuts have been removed, should be removable with hand pressure only.

A new 'Rotoflex' has a steel band around its periphery and this serves the same purpose as a compressing tool. The joint should be fitted with the long bosses on the bolt holes, towards their respective drive shafts: these act as spacers. Once all bolts have been fitted, the metal band should be removed from the coupling.

BLEEDING THE HYDRAULIC SYSTEM

Every car made today is fitted with hydraulic brakes in which movement of the brake pedal is transmitted to each brake by means of a liquid. Liquids are incompressible, so that there is no 'play' between pedal and brake. However, gases can be compressed, so that any air that finds its way into the system takes up some of the pedal movement and leads to a spongy feel. The greater the amount of air, the greater the loss of efficiency; eventually the state is reached where

should be jacked up and the wheel removed. Having made sure that the master cylinder is topped up with the recommended fluid, the bleed nipple should be loosened.

A rubber tube should be placed over the nipple, with its lower end in a jar of clean fluid so that air cannot be sucked in.

Depressing the pedal firmly and releasing it slowly will pump fluid and air out of the nipple. When air bubbles cease to appear at the end of the tube,

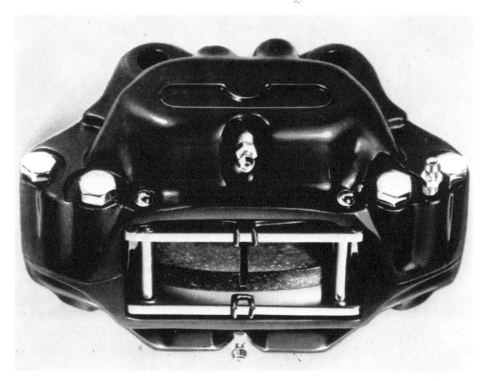

Right: a typical disc brake caliper, with its pads installed

Below right: if the brake pedal is pumped during bleeding and bubbles fail to leave the tube and enter the jar of fluid, then the nipple can be retightened

all braking will be lost unless the pedal is pumped.

All the hydraulic brake manufacturers allow for the removal of air by building bleed nipples into each wheel cylinder. By unscrewing these about half a turn, the air can be pumped out. The procedure for carrying out bleeding is fairly standard for all makes of car, although if a servo is fitted this will have to be bled separately.

If any of the brakes are drums, the adjusters should be tightened as far as possible before starting the air removal process. Starting with the brake farthest from the master cylinder, the car

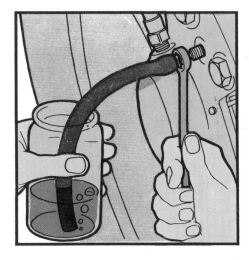

the pedal should be held down and the nipple tightened.

This procedure should be repeated at each wheel, topping up the master cylinder each time, working towards the cylinder. Finally the brakes should be correctly adjusted (free the adjusters until the wheels just bind).

It is obvious from the above description that this job requires two people. However, it is possible to obtain a set of special bleed nipples with valves which obviate the need for a tube and a jar of fluid. The only snag is that it

becomes a matter of trial and error to remove all traces of air. It is also possible to purchase an accessory which fits on top of the brake fluid reservoir, thus enlarging it. It is then filled with fluid and connected via a tube to the spare tyre, so that the system is pressurised. Thus there is no need for the second person to pump the pedal.

Fluid into which air has been passed should not be re-used, because some of the air will have been asborbed which will lead to further sponginess.

RENEWING HYDRAULIC BRAKE SHOES

If air has found its wy into the hydraulic system, there must be a reason for it. Unless there is a loose connection somewhere, the chances are that the air is leaking in round the seals in the wheel cylinders.

Usually, this leakage will be accompanied by a loss of fluid, indicated by dampness round the offending unit or components.

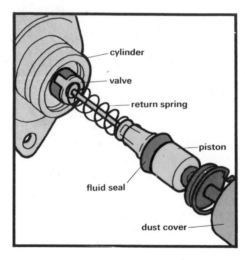

Right: the components of a typical master cylinder for a hydraulic brake system

Once the faulty cylinder has been traced, it should be removed. For drum brakes this means taking the brake drum off and removing the shoes before starting on the cylinder itself. Drum-brake cylinders are usually held on by a circlip or by a nut, and the hydraulic pipe should be unscrewed before the fixings are tackled. Discs are easier, since the wheel is usually all that need be removed before attention is turned to the cylinder(s) which are situated within the caliper. In most cases, the caliper is attached by two bolts, although, once again, the hydraulic pipe should be removed before the fixings are undone.

Disc-brake pads can be left in when removing the caliper, but it is best to remove them before reassembly, as they may catch on the edge of the disc.

Drum and disc-brake cylinders have a fundamental difference in that the fluid seals for a drum are fitted to the piston while that or those for a disc are fitted to the cylinder. However, servicing procedures are similar.

REPAIR KITS

Repair kits can be purchased for a small amount of money from most accessory shops. Thes comprise new fluid seals, new dust covers and any circlips or retainer necessary. There is often a tube of rubber grease supplied with the kit as well as a cover for the bleed nipple.

With drum-brake wheel cylinders, the piston or pistons (depending on whether the brake is twin or single-leading shoe) can be pulled from the cylinder. If there is any resistance, then the hydraulic pipe can be reconnected and the offending parts freed by pumping the brake pedal.

The cylinder and its pistons should be cleaned with a clean, dry cloth; any corrosion in the cylinder can be smoothed down by using fine abrasive

Right: a drum brake wheel cylinder exposed; a repair kit usually comprises any seals or dust covers for two wheels

such as metal polish. If the cylinder is scored or pitted, then new seals will

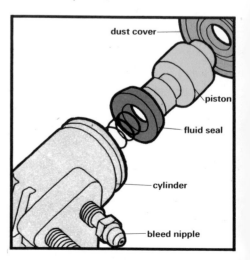

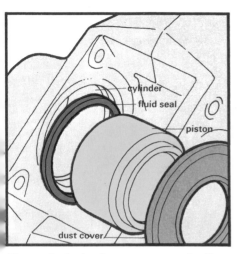

Above: the hydraulic components of a disc brake caliper

Right: two pictures showing removal of a spring retaining clip which holds the disc pad pegs in and the pad itself, together with a shim which is fitted to prevent brake squeal

Below right: the brake drum must be removed before the brake shoes can be inspected (near picture); sprung retaining clips may be used to hold the shoes in place, but often they are retained only by the return springs

not cure any fluid leak, the only answer being to replace the whole cylinder assembly. Having fitted the new seals, assuming the old cylinder is being retained, the parts should be liberally coated in new brake fluid of the correct type before they are reassembled. Don't forget to replace the dust covers which prevent dirt and moisture creeping between piston and cylinder and causing corrosion.

When fitting seals, be very careful not to overstretch them or break them; be especially careful if they are to be reused, not to cut them while using an implement to prise them out of their grooves.

Discs can be slightly more complicated. The manufacturers are firm in their recommendation that the calipers are not dismantled, so there is not much space in which to remove the pistons. Once again, should they stick, hydraulic pressure should free them, but perseverance is often the order of the day for this task.

The cleaning procedure is the same as for drum brakes, although seal-fitting is easier, because it or they fit in a groove or grooves in the cylinder wall. Pistons ars usually chrome plated, so if they are corroded they should really be replaced. They can be bought as separate items and are not expensive, although they may have to be obtained from a brake specialist.

Once the braking system has been reassembled and reconnected, the air will have to be removed, using the process already described. By the way, don't spill fluid on the paint, it is highly corrosive.

DAMPERS

Modern dampers (often wrongly known as shock absorbers) will usually last many thousands of miles before they require any form of attention. Early dampers used various mechanical friction devices as bases for operation, but all contemporary units offer resistance to movement by forcing hydraulic fluid through small holes.

If failure does take place, it is usually due to wear in an internal fluid deal. However, a seal in the casing may leak and allow all the fluid to leak away, thus rendering the unit inoperative.

It is important to maintain dampers in good condition as they are crucial to the safe handling of the car.

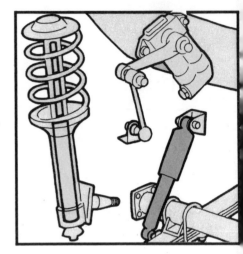

Right: three versions of the hydraulic damper – the normal telescopic unit (blue), the lever type (mustard) and the MacPherson strut variety (yellow)

TOPPING UP

There are two basic types of damper; lever-arm and telescopic (MacPherson struts contain telescopic dampers). The telescopic assemblies are, in nearly every case, sealed for life, so repairs are impossible, but lever-arm dampers can be dismantled for repair and can easily be topped-up with fluid. The fluid is specially formulated for use in hydraulic dampers and neither brake fluid nor lubricating oil should be contemplated as a substitute.

Dampers are never mounted rigidly at both extremities, even if at one. Lever-arm units are usually bolted firmly to the car body or chassis, with the end of the operating arm connected to some moving part of the suspension via a rubber or synthetic bush. Telescopic dampers can be mounted in the same fashion (especially if they are in unit with the springs) or they may have bushes at each end.

Right: the MacPherson strut suspension system used on the front of the BMW 520; this uses a telescopic damper located within the strut itself

Opposite page, below: further views of strut-type front suspension, together with diagrams of a coil-spring/telescopic damper set-up

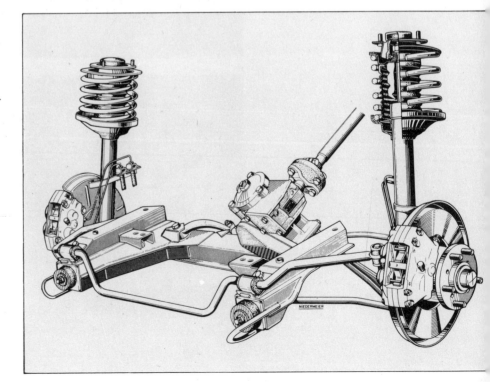

REPLACEMENT

Below: most telescopic dampers have rubber mountings to cut down the transmission of shocks and noise

If a damper breaks beyond repair, replacement is a simple procedure, unless the unit is combined with a suspension spring, bolts or nuts and bolts holding the unit to the car. In the case of spring/damper units, the whole assembly must be removed before using a special tool to compress the spring before replacing the damper unit.

With MacPherson struts, the damper portion can be replaced by using a new insert. This is usually held in by a knurled nut at the top.

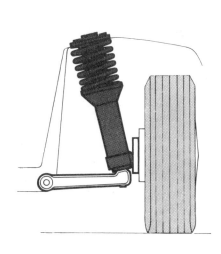

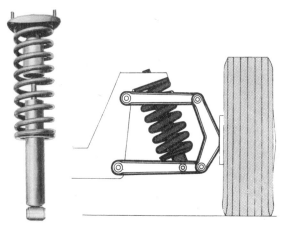

BODYWORK

ACCIDENT DAMAGE

Owing to a number of factors, including the soaring cost of skilled labour and constant increases in the price of spare body parts, perhaps the most expensive repairs carried out on the average motor car are those concerned with bodywork damage. These high costs and, in some cases, a low standard of finished work, are encouraging more and more private motorists to attempt to repair minor body damage themselves. This can, in many cases, be carried out quite successfully by a reasonably competent do-it-yourself man but it must be borne in mind that a modicum of skill, a lot of patience and considerable time must be spent on carrying out such work if a high standard of finish is to be achieved.

Furthermore, no attempt at rectifying body damage should be made unless a thorough study of the cause and effect of the incident responsible for the damage is carried out. Although body damage may appear to be only superficial to the untrained eye, a creased panel or a slightly buckled wing may hide a much more serious condition which is inherently dangerous to the performance and safety of the vehicle.

INSPECTION

If a car has received what appears to be superficial damage to the front or wing areas, a careful inspection should be made to ensure that the radiator has not been punctured or moved. Following this a careful check should be made on the water level at every opportunity to ensure that water is not leaking away through a badly fitting or stretched hose or from a damaged coupling. If the vehicle in question is fitted with a water temperature gauge this too should be checked; first of all to make sure that it is still in working order and then to ascertain whether the cooling system is still functioning at the same level of efficiency as before the incident causing the damage.

Yet another check may be instituted by inspecting the headlamp settings. If it proves impossible, or even just very difficult to set these correctly following what appears to have been a minor accident, this could indicate something quite serious, such as a twisted subframe or a deformed side rail in the vehicle's unitary body.

A careful study should also be made of the steering performance of the vehicle following minor shunts. If the steering should develop a distinct pull to one side, or be unable to hold a straight line when the driver removes

Near right: before repairing a scratch, clean the surrounding area with a cloth dipped in white spirit. This will remove any grease or wax which might prevent filler from 'keying' into the damaged part

Far right: mix a small quantity of filler paste and rub it across the scratch so that it completely fills the depression. Leave the filler standing slightly proud so that it can be rubbed smooth when dry. Use only a very fine grade of wet-or-dry paper and keep it wet to prevent cloggging

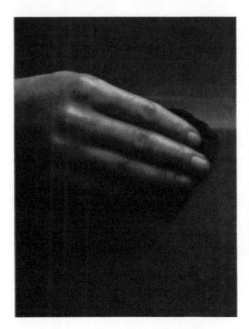

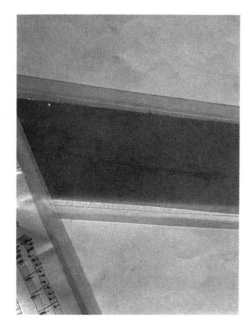

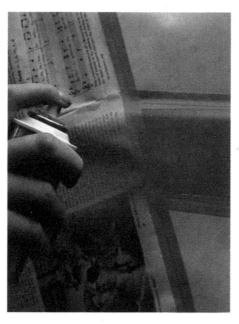

Above: once the surface of the filler is flush with the existing paint, mask the area surrounding the damage. Make sure the surface is dry before painting

Above right: apply two coats of primer before turning to the top coat. Once again, use wet-or-dry paper to smooth the paint between coats.

applied. Another check should be made for uneven tyre wear on one or both front wheels. If the steering geometry has been affected in any way, uneven wear should quickly manifest itself and the services of a proper garage be used to return the whole system to peak efficiency.

Other indicators that serious, though hidden, damage has occurred, include a badly fitting bonnet lid or passenger doors that do not shut without extra effort being applied or which, suddenly, do not match up with the striker plates.

A similar check should be carried out following damage to the rear section of the car. The boot lid should be checked for ease of action and tight fit. Uneven tyre wear should be watched for on the rear wheels also. A simple method of testing the rear-wheel geometry and brakes is to use only the handbrake to pull up the vehicle on a deserted stretch of road. As the modern car's handbrake usually works only on the rear wheels, any pulling to one side by the vehicle would indicate that a more thorough check should be made on the whole rear suspension and braking system.

CORROSION

his hands from the steering wheel, this usually indicates that some damage has been caused to the steering linkage or that the steering geometry of the car has been affected. Furthermore, the braking action of the car should still ensure that it pulls up in a straight line when the brakes are

Rust is another factor that should be considered when discussing body damage. Any rust appearing on the surface of a motor car's bodywork should be dealt with immediately by sanding away and then repainting with primer and a matching proprietary paint.

Body damage is not dealt with quite so easily, even though repairs are within the capability of most people, provided sufficient time and care is taken at each stage of the repair procedure. The equipment needed consists, usually, of an electric power hand-tool, a body file, some sheets of

rubbing down paper of various grades, a rubbing block, a screwdriver and a proprietary body filler kit which contains both the filler compound and a catalytic agent. For finishing the repair the usual method is to use aerosol cans of primer and paint, which are readily available.

It can be deduced from the above, that amateur body repairs do not involve the body straightening or panel beating techniques used by the professional. The main method for the amateur is to use the body filler to restore the original contour of the damaged panel.

REMOVING PAINT

The first step in a repair of this nature is to fit a coarse sanding disc to the power tool and use this to sand away paint, primer, dirt and rust from the damaged area until bare metal is showing. Care should be taken to sand right to the edges of the area under repair and just slightly into the surrounding, undamaged paintwork. After power sanding a medium grade of rubbing

paper should be fitted to the rubbing block and used on the metal to give a high degree of smoothness to the affected area. Touching the sanded area with the fingertips should be avoided as grease from the skin will prevent the filler compound 'keying' properly to the prepared area and could result in an unsatisfactory standard of finish.

FILLING

The next stage is to prepare the filler compound. Two main types are available: one is very hard when set and

the other softer and slightly flexible. The latter is the better of the two, as it is easier to sand and it withstands

Above: rust holes must be thoroughly cleaned before filling. If the back of the panel cannot be reached, the edges of the holes must be hammered in to allow glassfibre and resin to be used. Brush the edges with resin, then apply a glassfibre patch just larger than each hole, impregnating it carefully with more resin

Above right: when the resin is dry, filler can be applied to fill any dents

further knocks and vibration without cracking or falling out. A quantity of paste (perhaps half a small can, but dependent on the size of the area to be repaired) should be scooped out of the can and placed on a smooth working surface which is free from pitting or ridging — a piece of Formica is ideal. The paste should be spread out and the catalytic agent — which converts the paste into a hard setting, very tough and durable compound —

is added to the paste. The usual proportion is a half tube of the catalyst to a half can of paste.

Using the paste applicator, usually a piece of stiff plastic which is included in the filler kit, mix the paste and the catalyst with a smooth forward and backwards action of the wrist. This should be done in such a manner as to ensure that not only are the two parts of the compound mixed thoroughly, but also that any air bubbles trapped in the filler are eliminated. It is unwise to mix a great deal of filler at once if you are a novice, as it may begin to set, thus becoming unworkable, before you have finished.

Again using the applicator, apply the filler to the damaged area of the car, just a little at a time and spread in layers. Pushing the filler hard down onto the area, layers should be applied until the filler stands a little proud of the remainder of the body panel under repair. The filler should then be allowed to harden. Time taken for this varies and heat can be used to accelerate the process, but the longer a car can be left in a clean, dry atmosphere the better. Even so, two or three days is more than sufficient.

SMOOTHING DOWN

Right: the hardened filler can be shaped using a coarse file and smoothed down with wet-or-dry paper until it matches perfectly the body contours, leaving a smooth surface for painting

Once the filler has set, the high spots of it should be rubbed away. The first step in this process is undertaken with the special, but inexpensive, body file, which can be adjusted to conform to the curvature of the vehicle's contours. Following this, a medium grade of rubbing paper fitted to the rubbing

block should be used to smooth the repaired area and to feather the repair into the surrounding, undamaged areas of the vehicle's bodywork.

Once a smooth finish has been achieved — and in order to effect a really first class job — the repair should be left for at least a week, preferably two. After this, a final skim coat of the body filler is applied to the area after sanding down once more with a fine grade of wet-or-dry paper and then drying off thoroughly. The skim coat should be so thin as to allow the original filler to be seen through it and the purpose of this final coat is to fill in any small, and in some cases invisible, holes which might have appeared on the original surface.

Following this, and having allowed time for the skim to harden, the whole area should be rubbed down once more with a very fine grade of rubbing paper, used dry, and then finally finished off with an even finer grade of wet-or-dry paper, used wet and without the rubbing block, using light hand pressure only.

MASKING

After allowing this final skim coat to harden thoroughly, perhaps for another week, the repair is then ready for

painting. To do this, the area to be painted should be washed thoroughly with clean, cold water and then dried.

Brown paper and adhesive tape should then be used to mask around the repaired area in order to prevent over-spray affecting undamaged paintwork.

If working in the wing of the car the wheels and tyres should also be masked off; and if working near glass this too should be covered over.

PAINTING

Aerosol primer is then applied, the aerosol being held about 12 inches from the area to be sprayed and a forward and backward action is used, taking care to spray in a straight line and not with an arcing action. Allow the primer to dry and then rub down with a very fine grade of wet-or-dry

Right: the area to be sprayed should be masked, as with the scratch treatment, and then the damaged part sprayed with primer followed by several coats of finishing paint

paper, used wet. Wash the primed area and then allow to dry thoroughly. Paint should be applied in the same way as the primer but with the button of the aerosol being released at the end of each stroke in order to minimise paint build up.

A further coat of paint should be applied once the original layer has been allowed to dry quite thoroughly. Once the final coat has been applied, it should be allowed to dry for around three to four weeks. After this period, the surface of the repaired area should be rubbed down with a special compounding paste, again freely available from most good accessory shops. By taking care at this stage, the paint will be gradually polished to an acceptable level and, if all the steps taken have been performed correctly the repaired area of the bodywork should be indistinguishable from other areas of the car. Remember not to wax polish the surface until the paint is hard.

PANEL BEATING

If panel beating is required, then it is best for the amateur to beat the panel back until it is still slightly indented and then finish it off as above. Perfect panel beating is a highly skilled job.

Rust holes may have to be filled with glassfibre or something solid before filler is applied. In a hollow section, chicken wire can be inserted to provide a key, but where this is not possible, then glassfibre matting should be applied or expanded metal should be screwed behind the hole, using self-tapping screws or 'pop' rivets in countersunk holes. These holes can then be filled.

Near right: only a small amount of resin should be mixed with hardener at once as it sets quickly; to fill a split, resin should be applied to the back of the area after it has been throughly cleaned and plastic tape has been stuck to the front to prevent leakage

Far right: a piece of glassfibre matting large enough to cover the split and of a suitable grade should be cut and laid over the resin already applied (above); then more resin should be worked into the matting, using a stippling brush, until it is thoroughly impregnated; it should then be allowed to dry before filler is applied to the outside

EXHAUST

Right: a straight-through silencer; this type has a continuous pipe running through it and perforated within the silencer body; the wadding wrapped around it absorbs much of the noise generated by the pulsating nature of the exhaust

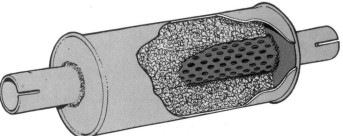

Unfortunately, no matter how well a standard exhaust system is painted, It will eventually corrode through. The reason for this is that it is not possible to paint the inside thoroughly and the exhaust gases contain extremely corrosive compounds.

One answer to this is to fit a stainless-steel system (these are commercially available), and the other is to use a metal coating, such as galvanising, on the surfaces of the parts. However, for the time being, the majority of car manufacturers use ordinary mild steel as the material for their exhaust pipes and silencers and this usually means at least a silencer-change every year or two and often a system-change at the same time.

FILLING WITH PASTE

There are several compounds on ths market which can be used to seal small leaks in pipes and silencers. These take the form of pastes which set rock-hard upon the application of heat. Larger holes require the use of patches and these can be either metal plates, made from pieces of scrap sheet, or special bandage. The paste is most useful for sealing leaks in the joints between two pieces of pipe — it tends to be blown out of anything other than pinholes in silencers or exhaust pipes.

FITTING A PATCH

Below: when using a repair bandage it is best to wrap a piece of foil around the leak first. Once the bandage has been applied plenty of wire should be used to hold it in place

Should a large hole develop in a silencer, the area around the hole must be cleaned before any repair can take place. This repair work is made easier if the silencer is removed from the car, but this procedure is usually not a necessity. Assuming the puncture is larger than a pinprick, paste should be applied around the edges of the hole before a metal plate, cut from something like a discarded oil can, is placed over it.

The plate can be fixed in place either with wire wrapped round the whole of the silencer body, or with self-tapping screws.

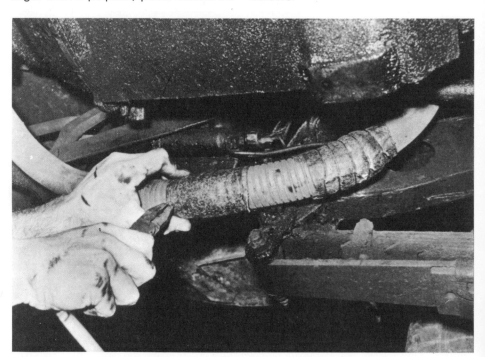

USING BANDAGE

If bandage is being used, the paste will be unnecessary. If the hole is a large one, a piece of tin foil, placed between the breakage and the bandage, will prevent the latter from being burned by the hot exhaust gases.

The bandage itself should be cut into strips large enough to cover the hole, and these should be over-lapped to give a firm repair. The patch should be held in place with wire, which is usually supplied with the bandage.

FLEXIBLE PIPE

Repairs to exhaust pipes should be carried out in the same way. Some cars use flexible pipe sections to allow for engine movement; these can be treated in the same way as ordinary pipe, but it will be a help to force paste into the grooves between the pipes. Because of the flexibility expected of these pipes, repairs to them are likely to be rather short-lived.

Flexible pipe is quite easy to obtain, in various sizes, and it is a straight-forward job to unclamp or cut off the failed piece and fit a new section.

Exhaust systems are usually suspended by flexible hangers and/or from rubber mountings. These often break, but they should be easily replaced by undoing the mounting bolts and fitting new ones.

Above and right: various types of clip and hanger are used; some, such as the one above, serve two purposes, while others, like the one right, are mountings only. In both cases, it is a good idea to renew all the parts when changing the exhaust system

REPLACEMENT

If new parts are required for the exhaust system, these cannot be fitted until the old ones have been removed. This job is often more difficult than it looks. If two exhaust parts are rusted together and cannot be freed by means of a hammer or any amount of pipe wobbling, then heat should be applied, by means of a blowlamp, taking great care not to damage any paintwork, brake or fuel lines etc, or to heat the petrol tank.

CUTTING SLOTS

The usual way to hold two pieces of pipe together is to fit one inside the other, providing the outer piece with slots to facilitate clamping. The heat should expand the outer pipe more than the inner, thus breaking the rust bond.

A new pipe may not have slots cut in it; if this is to be the outer part, these will have to be provided by sawing about two inches down from the end of the pipe, making at least two opposite cuts about 3/32 of an inch wide.

When the two parts are placed together, paste should be used to ensure a good seal round the joint. It is preferable to use a new clamp, tightening it until the slots close up enough to prevent the joint moving. In this way, the connections should last indefinitely.

LIGHTING

CLEANING

The correct fitting, maintenance and adjustment of lights is essential to safe driving at night or in fog. First of all, even if the whole vehicle is not cleaned regularly, the lights, both front and rear, should be wiped over with a damp cloth every week or so to ensure maximum efficiency. A layer of dirt over a headlight will cut its power by a surprising amount and will be inclined to spoil the carefully designed shape of the beam. In the case of a rear light, side light or winker, the same sort of dirt doverage could mean that in murky conditions another driver, whether following or approaching, may not see the vehicle.

Right: this photograph shows clearly the difference in effectiveness between standard tail lights and special bright fog lights, which are now standard on some cars

WASHERS AND WIPERS

Below: an exploded view of a typical sealed-beam headlight unit, in which the filaments are built into the reflector-and-glass unit

It is possible to buy washer/wiper attachments for the headlights; these are useful in slightly wet conditions.

Every time the lights are cleaned, they should be checked to make sure that all bulbs are functioning correctly. It will be a help if an assistant can check the stop lights, but this job can be carried out single-handed by reversing the vehicle until it is close to some slightly reflective surface such as another vehicle's bumper or a garage door. The number-plate illumination should not be forgotten, as failure of this sytem is a favourite excuse for the police to stop a car.

As far as the law is concerned, the requirements for car lighting in Britain are that there should be two bright white front lights, two red tail lights, two red stop lights (if these were fitted as original equipment on the car), a number-plate light and some form of indicator system — either two semaphore arms or four flashing lights.

Several other types of lamp are available on the accessory market: spot lights, fog lights, reversing lights, special bright tail lights for use in fog. Although none of these is a legal necessity, there are certain laws which relate to their use and fitting. Spot lights must either be fitted and used in pairs or be wired into the headlight main-beam circuit so that they cannot be used on their own. The same applies to fog lights, the reason being that a single front light is likely to be confused with that of a motor cycle by drivers of oncoming vehicles (the side lights tend to be obscured by the brightness of the main lights).

Reversing lights and stop lights must be no brighter than 24 watts and reversing lights which are not operated by the gear lever must have a warning light built into or near the switch.

Flashing indicators must operate at a rate between 60 and 120 flashes per minute, in order that they cannot be confused with any other type of lamp. They must also have a warning light to indicate when they are in use.

Headlights and spot and fog lights must be fitted a certain distance from

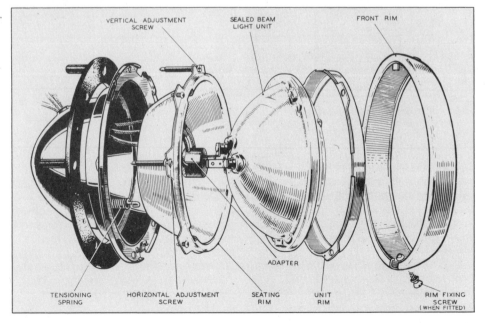

VERTICAL ADJUSTMENT SCREW   SEALED BEAM LIGHT UNIT   FRONT RIM

TENSIONING SPRING   HORIZONTAL ADJUSTMENT SCREW   SEATING RIM   UNIT RIM   ADAPTER   RIM FIXING SCREW (WHEN FITTED)

the ground. In the case of headlights on ordinary cars this is a minimum of 24 inches and a maximum of 42 inches. Fog lights can be mounted below 24 inches, but they must only be used in fog or when snow is falling; the maximum height is still 42 inches, which means that the roof-mounted spotlights seen on some 'rally' cars are illegal. Most auxiliary lights (spot and fogs) are fitted either by being bolted through the panel between the front bumper and the radiator (if there is one) or by being clamped to the grille itself on special brackets.

Spot lights should be adjusted to point straight along the road, as should main-beam headlights, unless they are going to be used with dipped beam headlights. Fog lights should shine down and in so as to cut reflection from fog, which occurs on high-beam, and to light the kerb as much as possible.

ADJUSTING HEADLIGHTS

On most headlights, adjustment is effected by removing the chrome-plated rim — this may have a screw in its lower edge — and turning one or both of the two screws, one at the top and one at one side. Adjustment of the top screw moves the beam in a vertical plane, while the side screw shifts the beam in a horizontal plane.

The vehicle should be parked on a flat surface, about twenty or thirty feet from a wall, and the main beams adjusted until they shine ahead straight and horizontal.

Near right: on older cars the headlamp rim must be removed in order to adjust the direction of the beam by means of two screws, one for horizontal movement (as here) and one for adjustment in the vertical plane. More modern cars are usually provided with adjustment either inside the car or behind the light unit

Far right: auxiliary lights can be mounted either through the bumper or panel behind it or directly into the radiator grille

REPLACING BULBS

Below: festoon bulbs, like this, are common in interior lights and usually have 'bullet' connectors

Replacement of bulbs is usually simply a matter of removing the lens from the light in question and taking the broken bulb out, either by unscrewing or by pushing, twisting and pulling as in a household bulb. However, some lights use festoon bulbs (cylindrical with a contact at each end) and replacement of these is easy and straightforward. Also, a modern trend is towards capless bulbs (all glass) and these are a push fit in their sockets.

Headlights and auxiliary lights are another matter. Most modern headlights are of the sealed-beam type, which means that if a filament fails, the whole of the glass unit has to be replaced. This involves removing the rim, unclamping the glass from its metal surround and unplugging the wires from the back. Some headlights do use bulbs and these are clipped in from the back.

If quartz-halogen lights are fitted, these can have either bulbs or, like headlights, sealed-beam units. Once again, if the sealed-type breaks, the whole unit must be replaced — this tends to be a particularly expensive task.

Quartz-halogen bulbs are clipped in either from the side of the light unit or from the back. It is very important removing or fitting one of these bulbs that great care is taken to avoid touching the quartz envelope: any moisture on the hands may cause the bulb to break when it heats up. Methylated spirits should be used to clean off any dampness.

Glossary

Alternator common type of electric generator on modern cars. Although it works by producing alternating current (AC), this is converted to direct current by a device called a rectifier.

Anti-roll bar steel bar connected to both sides of the suspension, so that if one side moves some of the movement is transferred to the opposite side. This helps to reduce the tendency to roll or sway when cornering.

Big end the end of the connecting rod which is fixed around the crankshaft. Thin shells lined with bearing-metal are fitted; if these bearings fail, one says, 'The big ends have gone.'

Block the main body of the engine casting, in which the cylinders are fitted.

Bore the internal diameter of the cylinders in which the pistons move to produce power.

Cam follower the part which rests directly on the cam and which transmits motion to the valve, directly in some designs but through pushrods and rockers in others. Several different designs are used.

Camshaft the bar of metal which carries the cams and which is turned by gearing from the crankshaft. The cams are usually egg-shaped in profile and give a to-and-fro motion to the valves as the camshaft rotates.

Capacity an indication of the size of an engine in terms of the amount of fuel-air mixture it requires, normally found by adding the swept volumes of all the cylinders. Usually expressed in cubic centimetres or litres.

Capacitor proper name for an electrical condenser.

Carburettor the complex system of tubes and jets through which the air passing into the engine is drawn and which delivers fuel in the form of vapour and droplets in the correct proportion for good combustion.

Clutch if no clutch was fitted the engine would stop whenever the car stopped. The clutch allows the drive to be disconnected and reconnected gradually; usually a friction plate connected to the wheels is clamped against the engine flywheel and released by a pedal.

Coil short for ignition coil, the device which provides the high voltage for the sparking plugs. An iron core has two coils wound around it, one fed from the battery, the other connected to the distributor.

Combustion chamber the space within an engine in which the fuel-air mixture is burnt. In a conventional car engine the combustion chambers are formed between the pistons and cylinder head.

Compression ratio indicates the number of times the mixture in a cylinder is compressed as the piston moves towards the cylinder head. Too low a compression ratio makes the engine less powerful and inefficient, too high causes detonation and engine damage. Most cars have compression ratio around 9 to 1.

Condenser small cylindrical box containing two sheets of aluminium foil rolled up together but insulated from each other. It is connected across the contact breaker (points) to improve sparking and reduce wear.

Connecting rod strong forged component, usually steel, which transmits the force from the piston to the crankshaft. It carries two bearings, one for the piston end called the small or little end, the other for the crankshaft and called the big end.

Constant-velocity joint swivelling joint in a shaft. In a front-wheel-drive car the use of such a joint is desirable to prevent jerkiness of the wheels when cornering.

Contact breaker mechanical switch operated by the rotation of the engine; when the contact is broken the spark occurs at the plug. Also called 'the points' although the surfaces are flat, not pointed. The contact breaker is normally within the distributor.

Crankshaft the main rotating part of an engine. It is driven by the connecting rods and drives the flywheel and gearbox. A pulley on one end also drives the water pump, the fan and the generator.

Crown wheel and pinion the pair of bevel gears fitted within the differential unit, which turn the drive through a right angle and transmit power from the high speed propeller shaft to the low speed half-shafts and thus to the wheels.

Cylinder the tube within which the piston moves. The cylinders are usually lined with wear-resistant cast-iron and carried in the top part of the crankcase, called the cylinder block.

Cylinder head the lid which closes the end of the cylinder and carries the valve gear and sparking plug. Most engines have a one piece casting forming a cylinder head for all cylinders together.

Damper a device which introduces deliberately a degree of friction or resistance to motion, so that rapid to-and-fro movement is reduced or prevented. Dampers are fitted to suspension systems.

Dashpot small reservoir of oil fitted on the top of a carburettor; it serves to damp out fluctuations in the movement of the carburettor slide and keeps the engine speed steady.

Detonation violent explosion of some of the mixture in an engine, due to overheating, maladjustment of petrol or too low an octane rating. Instead of burning progressively, the mixture ignites instantaneously to produce a shock wave which damages engine parts and can be heard as a high-pitched rattling noise called 'pinking' or 'knocking'.

Diesel engine which has no carburettor or sparking plugs, and in which combustion is produced by injecting fuel into air which has been compressed and heated within the engine. Diesel engines are more efficient than petrol engines but tend to be heavier, less powerful, and more expensive. Diesel fuel is more like paraffin (kerosine) than petrol.

Differential a special gearbox fitted in the transmission of a car so that drive is transmitted to both wheels on an axle whilst allowing them to rotate at different speeds for cornering. Most differentials consist of a nest of bevel gears driven from the crown wheel.

Distributor the device which connects the ignition coil to the sparking plugs in the correct order and at the correct time. Normally a rotor arm rotating within a plastic housing carries a brass sector which passes the high voltage to the High Tension leads in turn.

Final drive the means by which power is transmitted from the gearbox to the wheels. Shafts with constant-velocity joints are used on front-wheel-drive vehicles; rear-wheel-drive usually involves a central propeller shaft driving a differential to which the wheels are connected by half-shafts.

Four-stroke an engine of the conventional type used in motorcars in which four successive movements or strokes of each piston are necessary for one combustion cycle. They are: down, drawing in new mixture; up, compressing it; down after ignition, transmitting power to the crankshaft; up, expelling the exhaust or burnt mixture.

Fuel injection system used on all diesel engines and some petrol engines; instead of fuel being mixed with air in a carburettor, it is squirted under pressure into the inlet tract or combustion chamber.

Gearbox the range of usable engine speed of a motorcar engine is limited, and performance at low speeds is poor. To overcome these difficulties a gearbox is fitted so that the engine may be kept running at the best speed in any conditions. In most gearboxes a range of gearwheels offering different gear ratios is fitted, and the appropriate set is chosen by movement of the gear lever.

Horsepower old-fashioned way of expressing engine power, the rate of doing work or overcoming resistance. Engineers now work in kilowatts, which are less picturesque but easier to calculate and relate to other types of power.

HT leads the wires by which the high voltage is carried from the coil to the distributor and sparking plugs. HT is short for High Tension, an old-fashioned way of saying high voltage.

King pin the pin which carries the stub axle of a front wheel and allows it to be turned for steering. Not all cars have king pins as in some independent suspension systems they are replaced by ball joints.

Live rear axle in many cars the rear wheels are carried on a rigid assembly containing the differential and half-shafts. This simplifies design but such a live axle is ponderous and slow to react over rough roads.

Main bearings the bearings fixed in the crankcase in which the crankshaft turns. A modern four-cylinder engine may have three or five bearings; three are cheaper and lighter, but five give extra support for greater power output.

Master cylinder the cylinder in a hydraulic system to which a force is applied and which produces pressure in the system. Most cars have two master cylinders under the bonnet, one for the clutch and one for the footbrake.

Octane rating the resistance of a sample of petrol to detonation, which determines how suitable it is for use in an engine of a particular compression ratio. The higher the ratio, the higher the octane rating should be. In the UK it is indicated by a system of stars on petrol pumps; two-star fuel is a lower octane rating than four-star.

OHC overhead camshaft (see below).

OHV overhead valve (see below).

Overdrive the top gear which gives best performance does not give best cruising economy; an overdrive is an additional gearbox allowing the driver to choose the gearing to suit the conditions and to change rapidly from one to the other. The control is usually an electric switch.

Overhead camshaft Engine design in which the valves and their operating gear are fitted above the cylinder head, enabling high engine speeds to be produced, especially useful in engines with very small cylinders.

Overhead valve this term is used for engines with valves in the cylinder head operated by rockers and pushrods from a camshaft alongside the cylinder block. The design can be cheaper than OHC but is not as suitable for high engine speeds.

Pinking see Detonation.

Piston short closed cylinder of metal to which a force is applied to cause movement. In an engine, pressure on the light-alloy pistons from the burning mixture causes them to move in the cylinder, transmitting power to the crankshaft.

Piston rings circular bands of springy metal fitted into grooves around the top of a piston to seal against combustion pressure. They also help to remove heat from the piston and prevent oil from contaminating the burning mixture.

Pre-ignition fault in which the mixture in the engine is ignited for some reason before the spark occurs. The reason could be a flake of glowing carbon, an overheated exhaust valve, or an unsuitable sparking plug. On its own, pre-ignition only reduces power but it can rapidly lead to other problems, such as detonation.

Pushrods strong rods or tubes of metal connecting the cam followers with the rockers in an overhead valve design, so that the valves open and close as the camshaft turns.

Rocker metal bar fixed above the cylinder on a pivot near its centre so that an upward movement of one end causes a downward movement of the other. The pushrod causes the upward movement, the downward movement opens the valve.

Servo device which acts as a mechanical amplifier; a small applied force is augmented by the use of a separate supply of energy. In a braking system extra force is applied to the brakes by use of a large piston acted on by the partial vacuum from the engine inlet system.

Shock absorber common name for a suspension damper, although it is in fact the spring which absorbs the shock and the damper serves to dissipate the energy as heat.

Slave cylinder the cylinder in a hydraulic system which operates a component such as a clutch or brake; it converts the hydraulic pressure in the system to mechanical effort.

Small end the bearing of a connecting rod which moves within the piston and is connected to it by the gudgeon pin or wrist pin. The small end is also called the little end and is the other end of the connecting rod from the big end.

Solenoid electric device which uses the magnetic effect from a coil of wire to attract a bar of iron; this can be used to operate switches and move levers, as in many starter motors and overdrive mechanisms.

Splines grooves and ridges formed along a shaft or within a gear or similar component so that drive may be transmitted while sliding is allowed. Drive shafts are often splined so that the suspension can move without affecting the transmission of power.

Steering arms levers fixed to the stub axle of a front wheel and moved to and fro by the steering mechanism.

Steering rod steel bar or tube fitted with balljoints at each end, and forming the connection between the steering box and the steering arms.

Stroke the distance moved by the piston as it moves from one end of the cylinder to the other. A long stroke engine has a stroke greater than the cylinder bore dimension, a short stroke is less than the bore. If the two dimensions are equal the term 'square' is used.

Sub-frame an assembly of chassis parts often containing some mechanism which may be detached from the main chassis. On some front-wheel-drive cars the whole engine, gearbox, drive and steering mechanism are held in a sub-frame.

Sump the tray fitted to the bottom of the crankcase which seals it and carries the oil supply for the engine.

Swing-axles suspension design used in some smaller cars in which the rear wheels are carried on rigid drive shafts attached by universal joints to a fixed differential unit. Such a car can be recognised by the large changes in rear wheel tilt between the laden and unladen conditions.

Synchromesh mechanism fitted within a manual gearbox which ensures that the rotating gears are rotating at the correct speeds before they are engaged. Without such a device the gears would grate unless the driver were both skilled and careful.

Tappet old name for the cam follower used in side valve and some overhead valve engines. Adjusting or setting the tappets is the term commonly used for the adjustment of clearances in the valve operating mechanism even on engines which do not have tappets as such.

Torque technical term for the turning effect exerted by an engine. The power of an engine depends on the torque it produces and the speed at which it rotates. The gearbox and transmission gears reduce the speed of the driving parts so that plenty of torque is available at the wheels. Also an indication of the tightness required for a nut or bolt. Workshop manuals contain torque settings for all the important fasteners.

Torsion bar steel spring which takes the form of a long rod which is twisted. In some suspension designs torsion bars are attached to the chassis at one end; arms fixed to the other ends are connected to the wheels.

Track the width of a car measured from wheel to wheel, usually rather less than the overall width. A track rod is a steering rod connecting one wheel to the other so that the wheels always move together when cornering.

Universal joint one which provides for the transmission of power along a pair of shafts while allowing for mis-alignment of the shafts. Many designs are used; among those used for transmission purposes are constant-velocity joints and the Hooke joints common in many propeller shafts.

Wish-bones V-shaped steel components hinged to the chassis at one end and the axle assembly at the other, so that up-and-down motion is allowed while ensuring that braking forces are taken by the chassis. They are common components in many types of independent suspension.

Index